I0472670

Meditations on Meaning

in Life, Society, and Business

Babu P George, PhD, DBA

DEDICATION

To everything that kindled sparks of originality in me.

ACKNOWLEDGMENTS

A blank field can mean nothing; it can also mean everything.

PREFACE

Even though

When, In search of directions,
While wandering over the shores,
I saw that lovely little bird,
Flying across the mighty river,
And, I asked, upon my awe,
Where she was going,
With no doubt nor second thought,
Replied she, "to where my destiny is",
Then, asked me, where her destiny was,
And replied she, "where-so-ever my wings would fly me unto".

Yet

When your mind shuttles, restlessly,
Between east, west, north, and south,
It misses to see,
That all directions converge back,
Into the bosom of your very soul

And

That great chasm - deep, wide, and dark
Between words and what they stand for
Who, but the ones ready for a great leap of faith
Can ever hope to see that beyond, so glorious.

When that kind of a desire fires up in your soul, when you feel everything around you is telling 'you don't fit here', when you feel the past is roaring aloud to shed your baggage and rush forward naked, and when you feel the future is inviting you to help shape her, you will know your call in life. With that realization, my soul danced with it and my heart tickled my brain.

Ever since childhood, I am someone who wanted to live in the future. While accepting the reality of the present, it would not take me a quarter of 'the length of the present' to grow displeased with it and seek an imagined future. This constant discontentment did not mean I did not have an enjoyable life. Yet, most of the times I had enjoyable lives were when I lived in 'the illusory present of the future' or 'the fictitious present of the past'. The slices of personal reflections contained in this book will testify these.

Through these carefully selected samples, I have attempted my level best to express in the words of the world the rhymes and rhythms of my brain and heart. I humbly invite you to partake and celebrate with me these excerpts from the seasons of my soul.

Table of Contents

Thou shalt not (Always) Give Heed to thy Customers

Give heed to customers for ideas is strongly established and deeply ingrained as a key commandment in almost every version of the business bible. But, what if your best customers are with you just because you serve them with their conservative needs the best possible manner?

Would the best customers of Microsoft have told it that cloud computing was the future? No. Because, they are that conservative group whose traditionally well defined needs were being well met by Microsoft. If MS has moved on to 'software-as-a-service' model to some extent, it is because the software giant has looked over the shoulders of that huge innovation resistant group of its major office clientele. You can still hear their lamentations about how great Office 97 was in comparison with Office 365 and "how you would access Skydrive if you get shut off the internet?". Sometimes, innovation requires ditching your current customers.

Apple is the classical example of a company that cannot escape from its present customers. This is a sheer irony since we call Apple users as those celebrating themselves in golden cages and walled gardens. Apple is walled equally by its customers even as it continues to wall them. My prediction is that, if Apple continues this trajectory, it will soon become a brand for a niche group of mature (a.k.a. those who believe 'present is the future') customers - if it has not already become so!.

Google, on the other hand, is gifted with a strong customer base who like it for what it is rather that what one or a few of its current product offerings are. These customers are thirsty for a newer beta version of GMail every other month or less. They don't seek more of the same old wine. When Google introduces every new seemingly wacky product, or even when many such products are withdrawn after periods of languish, customers see them as expressions of a promise: a promise to feast them with innovations, one after the other.

Do your customers like you for who you are? Or, do they like you for what you currently give them? These are vital questions, answers to which should determine whether and in what measure you may give heed to them.

How the Anticipation of a Better Future can Age you Faster

Here is a scenario: I ordered a brand new iPhone 'x', which is expected to be delivered in a week. The specifications are fascinating, I am so much into it, and I want one week to pass in a wink. My intense anticipation makes me defocus myself from everything else that will happen over the course of this one week: I am alive but dead. Virtually, I time travel fast unto the delivery date. Then, the mailman knocks at my door with the packet of my brand new iPhone 'x'. Life is fun! What I don't realize, however, is that I lost 1 week from my life. In some way, I didn't live for that week.

The iPhone 'x' is just one of the many good things we expect in our lives. When the excitement of it is over, we will have one or more other anticipations. May be, I will want to drag to the present moment that future day the next year when I am going to graduate from the school. May be, I want to short the two weeks' time between today and the Spring break when I will be flying to Thailand with my girlfriend. Do we ever realize how many years from our lifetime these piles of anticipation take away?

Anticipation is well and good if it can somehow bring the future benefit to the present without taking away the time 'in between' from our lives. Say, my anticipation can motivate me to work harder to get an earlier pay hike or promotion. Not so much in the case of an iPhone 'x'. Unfortunately, most of our anticipations are of the iPhone 'x' type.

You may say, anticipation of good things can help us divert our attention from depressive experiences associated with the present life. May be true. But, it can also give us an illusory sense of happiness, as a result of which we don't get to address the root causes of our present misery. Overtime, these miseries pile up and attack us even more vigorously, as we want to continue to hide ourselves in other anticipations.

So, don't try to bring the future to the present any faster than it would reach you in its natural course. Rather, if you are currently going through bad tidings and if there is no practical way to tackle them, try to gracefully accept them. This will result in the perception of dilation the actual time – and, consequently, a feeling of the alleviation of your miseries.

A Few Overlooked Leadership Lessons, from 'The Wizard of Oz'.

On an otherwise dry but windy autumn's Sunday evening, while sitting by our Kansas home bored, my five year old daughter brought to me her tablet - asking me to watch with her the five minutes long cartooned version of the Wizard of Oz. I gave her the company she needed. Now that she left me to do the other things that interested her, I am back to my world of idealized reflections.

The story of the Wizard of Oz has for long attracted the attention of leadership experts. However, the story has almost always been used as a demonstration of existing and known leadership theories. It occurred to me that this is an injustice to its true spirit. In fact, the story demolishes the extant wisdom on leadership, on various counts. While it is "just a story", there is nothing that would make its underlying counter-intuitive ideas of leadership impractical in the real world. Let me highlight just five of these ideas here:

No, leadership does not need shared goals. The scarecrow wanted brain, the tinman wanted heart, and the lion needed courage. Many people who analyze the story will highlight a common goal for all the participants: i.e. to meet the wizard. But, that is not really the goal. Also, remember, Dorothy didn't beg people to help her find her lost home. It was each one on their journey, but together.

'Leader' is the personification of an idea that emerges in the leadership process. It is not the individual. What happens in our attempts to find a figurehead leader is to lose track of the *combined spirit* of all participants in the process. This combined spirit is *borne* by the tinman, the scarecrow, the lion, and Dorothy, from time to time, according to the particular situation. In the story, we are tempted to place Dorothy as the leader of the team. She did lead during a part of the process; but, so is every other team member. Everyone did their part to lead and follow.

A wizard is useful, not as a wish giver but as a spiritual mentor. While the scarecrow exercised its brain's potential, the tinman mellowed its heart up, and the old lion showed what true courage is all about, neither of them *realized* these. It needed the wizard. That said, trusting the wizard had a great motivational effect upon the compatriots on the journey. So is the good 'Witch of the North': this elderly but beautiful witch appeared in the story only for a momentary display, but had a lasting impact.

Don't look for strong followers. People's weakness is often their primary motivation to join you and work with you. And, don't underestimate anyone -

just because they don't possess a particular strength. This lesson should not be forgotten, as your follower selection process is full of wonderful tests of strength. Very valuable, when you hire someone for a job!

The achievement of leadership journey does not need to come from a destination. Leadership goals are often achieved during the journey, as people with divergent goals work collaboratively. No, it is not the mighty wizard.

Inspire and people will join you so they could each realize *their* own dreams. Dorothy did just that. Also, if a leadership role is thrust upon you, just make yourself available for it. I am reminded of the words of the Biblical God: "I am looking for your availability and not suitability".
Additional thoughts?

Why Organizations Need Imperfect Employees

In summary, human nature is just like that.

Will you want to be with coworkers who know everything as good as you (no mention, better than you)? Successful organizations are clamped together with the glue of employee imperfections. In an organization with every employee capable of doing equally well at everything will collapse down in no time. I know this is counter-intuitive, but wait before judging.

At one stage in life, I had the opportunity to work with three wonderful research assistants. Each of them was excellent in certain useful ways. One did a superb job as a questionnaire designer, one as a telephone interviewer, and one as a data analyst. Each of them had average skills in various allied aspects of conducting social research. They worked as a great team. I had no difficulty in appeasing their performance as superlative, despite their relative lack of skills in certain areas.

As a consultant, I have met with situations in organizations where every team member was equally smart at everything the team was expected to do. It was not that there was no division of work nor that anyone would encroach into the assigned responsibilities of others just because he could do it as well. The mere, simple, plain, awareness among team members that other members knew equally well what they were doing made them feel like pawns in the game.

With these experiences, I learned that every employee wants to feel that he is better than most others, at least in a few matters of importance in relation to his job. Every employee needs to justify his existence by convincing himself and others of the unique value he brings to the workplace.

We do need some awkward people in every social situation to make other people feel charming. What is important is that one person does not feel awkward in every situation and that the responsibility of awkwardness be shouldered on a rotational basis across occasions (if there are not enough naturally awkward people already there!). Someone or the other has to pretend imperfect, all the time.

The Man who Knows Everything is not an organizational man.

The Science of Likes, Comments, & Shares on Social Media

Is he your influencer because you like his posts? Or, you like his posts because he is already ordained as an influencer?

I remember as a school boy how our History teacher fooled us. He divided the class into three sections, gave an excerpt from a speech to each of the sections: To the first he said it was by Hitler, to the second it was by Martin Luther King, and to the third it was by some largely unknown African warlord. While the speech was originally delivered by Hitler, the differences in the way each of the sections responded were extremely striking and educative.

Male users of Facebook often jokingly complain that women get more likes, comments, and shares (LCS). Given the casual nature of most Facebook posts and the triviality we attribute to them, we care about such 'biases' only as a matter of light fun. However, it is not equally digestible when we see a similar trend in LinkedIn Pulse posts, where expectation is that knowledge be valued for its face value rather than the face value of the communicator.

It is curiosity inspiring to notice how anointed influencers or 'business leaders' who occupy high corporate offices getting thousands of likes, hundreds of comments, and tens of shares for their otherwise crappy-lousy posts. If you anonymize the identity of the author and share the same posts, you will know the difference in the LCS feedback.

Why are these biases? It could be one or a combination of the following:

Get noticed: The thinking is often like "what better way for me to possibly get noticed by Bill Gates than to comment on his posts". It does not take a lot of strain to notice that many of those who LCS the posts of a company's CEO are the employees (or, aspiring employees) of that company. Some LCS for celebrity posts can happen also because of our intuitive sense that "if I comment on some Harry's posts, no one may notice it and it is a waste of my efforts".

Self image boost: A lot of people who LCS influencers' posts may have a liminal experience of becoming part of an aspirational group to which those influencers belong. The esteem can reach its pinnacle when you post critical comments on such posts and in return you get multiple likes and mentions for the said comments.

Self marketing: Associated with the aforesaid elevated experiences of self worth, projecting to one's friends and colleagues that "I belong to the same league of thought of such influencers" is rewarding from the point of view of self-marketing, too.

Expert guidelines for LCS suggest that audience interest is more likely if you present original and interesting ideas, pose counter-factual possibilities, use clear writing styles, relate with the audience, and actively respond to reader comments. But, evidently, that's not all.

Finally, the open question: *Why do people (including me, the non-influential crowd) create new posts on LinkedIn and other social sites? For similar reasons as the ones listed above?*

O Employer, thy Craving for that Perfect Resume!

So, employers, ask yourselves: what are you looking for? Increasingly, it looks like you are seeking the best resume hackers out there. It looks like, for every job there, there is an ideal resume: those who can hack their resumes so as to make them resemble that ideal (or, those who can afford to pay a professional resume hacker to do that) are IN during the preliminary round of the race. Irrespective of their job hacking excellence.

Excellent candidates who do a 'poor' job in crafting a stereotypically perfect resume are a lost sheep! They soon get that chill-toned letter beginning with "Thank you for your ... After careful consideration, we are sorry to ... We wish you the best!". This happens often before a human agent could see them, as a result of automated filtering. Their loss?

But, dear employer, is it any less of YOUR LOSS? Are you not the one losing out more by your sheer ill-luck not to get some of the best candidates? Funny, most recruiters, HR managers, and hiring unit heads, do not think it is their loss that they could not filter in a superb candidate who did not have an equally superb resume. That's what LinkedIn columnists too lament about. It is as if, those who cannot perfect their resumes do not deserve a job - their qualifications for the job are a mere secondary.

Well, to be fair, though not often, we do get to hear how a deceiver-of-resume got into the ship - and put deep holes in that ship, to everyone's peril. A little more often, we also hear how some of the great souls, rejected by the top three or five employers in an industry emerge as champions elsewhere. These are the people who stir an industry's dynamism.

Blind elimination of candidates based on the merits of a two page resume or a five minute multimedia presentation is not as economical as most employers tend to think. It is crucial to realize that the ability to craft an ideal resume is not always in the natural instincts of many of our best employees. Success lies in a recruiter's ability to see merits despite a shabby resume. Stop taking pride in rejecting candidates because they did not know how to write resumes than because they did not know the job!

'Alma Mater Discrimination': Apply for this Job Only if you Went to Oxbridge

Dated October 6, 2014, the following advertisement appeared in the Chronicle of Higher Education.

We are looking for academics in any business disciplines at the assistant/associate/full professor levels.

Imperative requirements:

. A PhD from UK, US or Australian University OR a university in the top 100 in the Times Higher Education Ranking.

. Published papers in highly-ranked international journals.

The above requirements are imperative. Do not apply if you don't fulfill them.

I wish to specifically highlight the part that says "A PhD from UK, US or Australian University".

None of the Ivy League schools accept more than 10% of the applicants and hence the intent of such advertisements is prima facie evident. But, are advertisements like this not employment discrimination by another name? Filtering graduates based on their "UK, US or Australian University" tag smacks of prejudice. The demand that a student's association with the geographical location of a university should or should not accord him privileges merely camouflages old fashioned discrimination typologies. For example, locational disadvantages (and no less financial difficulties!) prevent certain traditionally underrepresented groups from getting admission to such institutions - irrespective of their intelligence or interest levels.

It is in everyone's wisdom that many of the universities in the above classification do admit students on 'payment seats'. I would say, it is far easier to get admission to an average Australian university than to an average Indian university - if your dad can financially afford it. Also, the graduation rate in most of these institutions is close to 100%. So, are not employers who make advertisements like the one posted above also (kind of) declaring that "apply for this job only if you managed to get admission for a certain educational program in such and such universities"? Shortlisting candidates for a job based on whether one had qualified for (discriminated) admission to a university is no less discriminatory.

The New York Times cartoon that (apparently) came out of the elitists' shock about the success of India's Mars mission has invited a lot of criticism from various quarters. For many, sari clad brown women scientists leading a mission like this was possibly unimaginable. And, in their attempt to scoff at this indigestible fact, they probably got scoffed at. For a fact, many  Asian universities are leading silent experiments in carving out a new breed of future-fit individuals, despite their resource limitations. There is no dearth to scientists, engineers, and artists who migrated to the West and made it to the top, after their schooling in some of these under-recognized Asian hamlets. Discrimination based on a candidate's particular School affiliation, although not illegal, could turn out to be suicidal for employers who pursue them. Better stay way!

A Rant on the Politics of Research Vs the Philosophy of Science

Irrespective of your disciplinary orientation or the field of inquiry, one thing that baffles you (or, does not baffle you anymore due to its triviality) is that research findings are getting refuted at a faster pace than ever before. So, in business research, yesterday someone proved that employee satisfaction led to employee loyalty, today someone else (or, may be the same researcher) not only refutes it but also proves that satisfied employees are more likely to switch jobs.

Earlier this month, PLOS ONE published a paper by a researcher that refuted the findings of a previous research published in the same journal by the same researcher. While one could argue that this is exactly the way science should progress, it is not easy to hide how the political nuances associated with the research enterprise, especially the politics of grant funded research, contribute to such developments.

Typically, researchers expect a particular result, based on prior theory (in practice, this often boils down to 'common sense'). They experiment, experiment, and experiment, until the observations fit with the expected results. While they patent the findings or while applying for grants for further studies, they never report the failed experiments or experiments that do not fit with their funding agency's 'vision of truth'. Among social science researchers who churn out papers based on survey results, the equivalent thing is to 'clean data'. Anything that does not contribute to the preconceived findings are outliers that needed to be weeded out. In the academic world, this makes a lot of sense: imagine, you spend an year on a research project, a paper based on the positive findings of which will determine your tenure in the university. Imagine the tussle between ethics and realpolitik!

In the competitive enterprise to produce research papers and amass citations, the more the merrier. So, if the same researcher can prove something, publish it, disprove it later, publish it again, that is double reward. To be smarter, why not hide a small fraction of your experiment (that could tilt the results) from the first paper and then introduce it to make a second path breaking paper! Thus, having dedicated journals to publish results refuting previous findings also might not be of much help.

Based on my own experience with social research, I can say that social science journals have largely become mediums through which academic communities self-sustain their egos. Business research journals are at one extreme: very rarely have practicing communities gained any substantial input from such mediums. Still, we the academic minded ones, keep publishing in them - because, that is what we are taught to do, we are supposed to do. I can understand the inadequacies of positivist methods and the unrealism in expecting universal generalizability when it comes to human and social science. But, the above-mentioned issue is not so much to do with the problems of the scientific method as it is with researchers not following it in their research conduct.

Solution? Well, I indicated in the title of this article itself that this would just be a rant. By the way, do any of you have a solution.

George, Babu P.

Loyalty out of Traumatic Bonding: Stockholm Syndrome in Customer Behavior

Yes, the internet is filled with haters of monopoly big businesses. But, no doubt there are big time fans for these businesses, too. I chatted with an old friend of mine today, who churned out numerous adjectives of praise for one such cable-internet-telecom company that served his hometown.

I got curious because this company enjoys a national dis-reputation in the US for the worst-class-ever customer service. What might explain the behavior of my friend and thousands just like him?

A rare act of kindness from this company - that it refunded him most of the cost of replacement of a router equipment after he was wrongly charged for it - led to his shower of praise. No mention he called their helpline for months to resolve this issue, no mention he drove to their local business office multiple times and waited in the long queues to highlight the issue, no mention their third-world internet speed and top-of-the-world usage fees, and no mention their universal panacea for all technical issues is 'disconnect, wait, and reconnect'.

Is my friend in a hostage situation? There is no other cable company serving his hometown, it is an essential service for him, and may be even a rare show of limited kindness is sufficient to inflame in him a plethora of positive feelings. Is not his empathy and sympathy for the cable company in question a special case of well studied and well documented Stockholm Syndrome? I believe so, strongly.

His feelings are irrational for people like us who view the situation 'out-of-context'; but, given the constant victimization endured, it is quite understandable why customers like him mistake occasional lack of abuse from their captor businesses for genuine acts of kindness. Customer loyalty to the perpetrators of crime: or, Stockholm Syndrome in customer behavior.

The Dumbness and Disutility of Personality Tests

Folks love personality tests. Check your Facebook notifications to count how many "how well do you seduce women?" quiz requests you receive every day.

An executive MBA student of mine who is also the human resource head of a company in Turkey says the only reason he uses personality tests is to weed out psychopaths and sociopaths. My counter question to him was: If someone is not smart enough to answer interview questions in a manner that would camouflage the psychopath in him, is he psychopath enough?

Well, my question may seem dumb, given all the scientific connotations attached to some of these instruments. Most reputed employers use some or the other form of these tests during their candidate selection process. The test results are used to judge whether the candidate is the best fit for the job and the business.

Now, something more silly: it doesn't require you to be a psychopath or a student of psychology to finish these tests successfully. You just need to tell some lies. Well, let me moderate: you just need to be smart enough to judge the expectations of the business and the personality of your interviewer. Isn't that just understanding your clients by putting yourself in their shoes? Simple trick of empathy? Even though you may not know the right answer, a little intuitiveness will help you weed out the undesirable answers posted to you. Say, for the position of a software development team member, if you are posed the work aptitude question "on a scale from 1 to 10, where do you stand as a team player", you should be able to weed out options 1 to 5 without much thought.

Finally, even if someone is a psychopath, why should you discriminate him against the 'normal' folks as long as he does not violate norms? Why should that matter, even if he may not have the empathy to support his pro-social behavior? Should someone's superior IQ not be utilized, as long as he is not a dumb psychopath who cannot hide his deeper drives? At another level, what if psychopaths are superior individuals who can rationally choose the best contingent response in a situation while 'normal' folks dumbly fall into a natural default answer with no sense of choice?

I do not deny the scientific value of personality tests. But, a job seeker is not so much interested in figuring out whether he is an introvert as he is in communicating to his potential employer that he is a desirable candidate. As I see it, the only remaining utility of personality focused screening tests is for the candidates to self-assess their degree of fitness. Let the employers encourage the candidates to take these tests anonymously and compare the test outcomes with the desired outcomes in order to see the gaps. It should end there for the unfit candidates, except if they still wish to remain in the race, with the hope of getting selected for the job and ruining themselves!

Against Method(ism) in Scientific Research

While I am not a fan of epistemological anarchism, there is some merit in Feyerabend's critique of the *method*. Our doctoral students are taught that method is everything, there is a single right (scientific) method, and that the right method ensures the right findings. When you write your research papers, you sequence the research process in such a manner that the method you chose made all the difference. I will, however, argue that method cannot be a substitute for understanding. Rather, the level of preconceived understanding supported by a particular method might promote or demote that method - except in those rare occasions when *paradigm shifts* happen in a discipline.

To make things simple, let's talk about this widely known relationship in the consumer behavior literature: Satisfied customers are loyal. Doctoral students will like to propose this as "there is a significant positive relationship between customer satisfaction and customer loyalty". What is *the right* method to test this relationship?

Let's assume that, in our universe, there are infinitely large number of possible methods to test this relationship. You randomly pick up one of these methods. How do you know if the method picked up by you is valid? The quality of a tree is known by its fruits. If the finding of the study is such that satisfaction does not predict loyalty, notwithstanding any grandiose idea that you may have about methodology, the first suspect will be your choice of method. A method that does not support the existing wisdom or expected relationships is a prime candidate for being trashed.

What we are taught in schools is that method is a higher level of truth. In the practice of science, however, method is subservient to the theory of particular disciplines that use it.

If the method chosen by you for the above study has a sustained track record of use in the disciple, the method is not easy to trash. The method has been deeply ingrained in the research practice in that field of inquiry; plucking the method away will raise questions about many other research findings fundamentally constituting that discipline, too - because, most of these findings were derived making use of this method. Needless to say, this is a serious concern for the gatekeepers of any discipline. So, the attempt will be to find *reconciliatory solutions*. How about this: Customer satisfaction did not result in customer loyalty *because* 'X' (X= Consumers globally are becoming more and novelty seeking, irrespective of satisfaction; Consumers don't have choice, so they exhibit the same repurchase behavior irrespective of their satisfaction level; etc). If the method supports these reconciliations, it becomes even dearer in the discipline. After all, in the present example, this method has helped with enriching the theory of consumer behavior!

A few of the alternative scenarios are more worth pondering. If the above reconciliation is offered by a nascent, relatively underused method, that method will also begin to gain traction. Over a time, it could become a popular method - even as a replacement for the previously held dominant method. On the contrary, if a nascent method fails to arrive at the reconciliation expected by the arbiters of the discipline, it is probably doomed forever. The most interesting scenario is when the originally mentioned well entrenched method too fails to support with the reconciliation. This could begin to brew a revolution in the discipline, in accordance with the grip that method has developed in the research tradition of that discipline. So, there is indeed a point at which a method is treated above the theory of a discipline that patronizes it.

Yet, the above mentioned success of method over theory should not be celebrated. It is dangerous in that truths that stand outside the purview of that method are now even less likely to be accepted. Fortunately, if history of science is an evidence, there is still hope. At certain rare junctures, youthful researchers with fresh ideas and indomitable zeal, who have glanced glimpses of the greater truth a-methodically in their creative minds, who dare to challenge the dominant figureheads of the discipline, who have no lucrative university positions to lose but their life's singular passion to win, appear from the tangents, for the epic fight. Not all of them succeed, but light cannot always be hidden under the bushel: the righteousness of the truth that they seek will declare them winners. Galileo and Einstein were made fun of, degraded. But, their truths won. Scientific progress is a treasonous struggle. It is a treacherous fight with what the *dominant design* making up the contemporary scientific practice deem as the right theory and the right method.

Note: This is an excerpt from the lecture notes of a PhD Seminar that I developed for business research students, several years ago.

Chaos - Order = Greater Chaos. Appreciate Complexity. Don't Reduce it.

Alright, let me present central argument of this piece. *Subtracting order from a chaotic system will only increase the chaos of the system.*

Think of a system 'S'. This system has an amount 'C' of chaos.

Now, let's assume we identify a sub-system 'S1' within 'S' that is more orderly.

The amount of chaos in it is C1, such that C1<C2.

The sub-system 'S1' is a layer of 'S'. A more predictable and better manageable layer.

We human beings have a natural urge to focus on 'S1' because it follows order and discount all but 'S1' as sporadic noise. Remember, we see cycles in the weather, in the economy, etc, and un-notice observations that do not fit into the anticipated patterns. What's more, in the short term, our predictions about 'S', based on the orderliness we see in the 'S1' *layer of truth* do come true. But, not for long! Commonsense fails us here.

When we extract away 'S1' from 'S', the amount of chaos in the remaining part of the system, let's name it 'S3', is C1-C2. Commonsense would say, C1-C2 should be less than C1. In the special scenario that C=0 (i.e., the sub-system 'S2' is a 100% deterministic system), C1-C2 should be equal to C1. But, it is never greater than C1. Again, as I said above, commonsense fails us!

Chaos theory says that C1-C2 is actually greater than or equal to C1.

In simple terms, *when we take away a certain degree of orderliness from a complex system, what will remain is a system with an even greater degree of disorderliness.*

I am not a climate scientist and my understanding of chaos theory is largely conceptual. Also, my research is mostly in business organizations. What I see often is managers downplaying the inherent complexity of organizational systems, identify certain layers of order that stand out, predictably model that order, and then manage based on it. They do not understand that the order they see is the tip of a chaotic whirlwind. It is easy to use that order as a tool to win support and to leverage power. Then, all of a sudden, the quake hits, invariably.

The root cause of many of our problems is our discomfort to live amidst chaos. We build artificial boundaries to create safe zones, thinking we have successfully isolated ourselves from the dirty and the devil. That doesn't solve anything but rather gives us an illusory sense of control. A very temporary respite, before something even more chaotic strikes at some of our most unexpected moments. The reductionist sense of control that we seek ultimately fails us. *What we need to develop is the stamina to appreciate the beauty of complexity in all its darkness and the consciousness to make sense of complexity without artificially reducing it. The scientific method should marry the poetic method, in order to resolve without reducing.*

The Classroom outside the Classroom: An Excerpt from my Early Childhood Experiences

I was born and raised in the rural countryside of Kerala, India. While I was a primary school student, during the first hour in the morning, I remember, I was asked by my class teacher to go and fetch for her a dozen of eggs from a farmer who reared ducks (not uncommon in rural public school settings those days). I, a seven year old boy, along with my friend and classmate Shiju, soon ventured into the task. Obviously, we both were to miss most of that day's classroom proceedings.

The farmer Mr. Kunjappan lived a mile away from the school. There was no paved road leading to his farm-home. Actually, there was no paved road passing through my village those days. Also, the teacher did not know where exactly the farmer lived but rather assumed that we would ask around and find our way out. We crossed many small streams of water, paddy fields, and swamps in search of the farmer. On the way we encountered various forms of wild life, from beautiful butterflies to a few no-too-funny snakes. We met peasants and farm workers who gave us clues to find out Mr. Kunjappan's whereabouts. We observed how women planted semi-grown rice plants in the fields and sang along with them the songs heralding the spring season. And, O the occasional drizzles and the pristine fragrance of that breeze that came to lull us often! We also jumped into the muddy fields (with the hope of) steering the ox-pulled plowing axes. If only Mr. Karthullil Kunju, the ox owner, was a little more empathetic to our lofty desires! After a walk that lasted around an hour and a half, we reached an area of cocoa plantation. No sooner, we began to hear from the other side of the plantation the quack-quack sound of a flock of ducks.

While we met Mr. Kunjappan, he was feeding his cows. He went inside his farmhouse and brought the eggs. Although we asked him to give us a dozen eggs, we did not know a dozen meant twelve until he counted up to twelve and said "here goes a dozen". He placed the eggs into a cushion made of dried banana leaves and reminded us to handle the eggs carefully. We gave him three one rupee coins that the teacher had given us. He counted them and told us something to the effect that the egg prices have gone up (well, not quite like the modern day corporate leaders: he lamented to us how the fodder prices have gone up, his family's living expenses have gone up, etc). We promised him that we would inform our teacher accordingly and he too agreed that it was okay to pay the remaining amount during the next trip. At that moment, his wife came out overhearing our conversation. She (lovingly) cursed him for talking about price to little kids and more so when the buyer of the egg was a school teacher and not a trader. She said she knew our moms and gave us two eggs each as a free gift to our moms.

We walked back to the school. Now that we have a better sense of the geography and that we had sensitive eggs to take care of, we decided to try out another route. We saw the first signs of 'development': the work to gravel that countryside path had just begun. We reached back at the school sometime after the lunch break got over. Given the boiled plantains we had from Mr. Kunjappan's home, pieces of chili-coconut flavored boiled tapioca we had from the farm workers, and the myriad wild berries we got to eat on the way, we were not really hungry though. We handed over the eggs to the teacher and told her about the debt she owed to Mr. Kunjappan. In the evening, I reached back home with the unopened lunch box, gave my mother the free eggs Mrs. Kunjappan gave, and told her the whole story. She was very happy. My dad was not equally impressed. He muttered but not much since the story involved, again, a teacher, a figure not far less respectable than a god.

Did I and my friend Shiju miss that day's class? (I remember, I could not name a spoon a spoon when John Sir showed me a spoon the very next day in the class and asked me in Malayalam, our local vernacular, what it was called in English). Or, were we privileged to spend a day in a much more open and marvelous classroom specially organized for us by the collusion of nature and society? An excerpt from my early childhood formative experiences - obviously, with factual errors most of which could be attributed to fading memories.

The Story of Sanjay and Sameera: Episodes in Cross-Cultural, Cross-Sectoral, Competence

It always amazed me how quickly Indians who land in a foreign country adapt themselves with the alien culture. Probably, there is no country in the world where people of Indian origin have not migrated and carved out success stories. Personally, I have come across many such success stories and the story of Sanjay and Sameera (names and some details anonymized) has particularly attracted my attention. Let's meet the family of Sanjay and Sameera as they continue their strivings to adapt themselves to the changing demands of a fluid, dynamic, but globally interconnected work environment.

Early Days in India

Sanjay and Sameera were born and brought up in India. Sanjay married Sameera in 2005 while he was working as a programmer for Infomatix, a Bangalore based multinational outsourcing company. At that time, Sameera had just graduated with an undergraduate degree in computer science from a college located in the hinterlands. She was handicapped by her poor command over the English language; also, she was ill-equipped for tech jobs due to the fact that her rural college taught her only arcane things. After multiple rejections, she got the job as a trainee software engineer for Kawavi, a Chinese based tech giant, in its Bangalore based software development facility.

Seeing the World through China

Despite an initial shock, she realized that it was much easier to work for Kawavi than to work for a similar company based in the US. For one thing, most other employees Kawavi recruited were from similar backgrounds that Sameera had. They had employees from many countries, mostly located in the East and the South East Asia – no one of them had great fluency in English. Also, given the uniqueness of jobs Kawavi engineers were expected to do, prior knowledge did not play as much a role as on-the-job training that they would give to new hires. These two things actually increased the empathy among the employees and they helped each other in every possible manner. During late 2006, Kawavi sent Sameera to Shanghai for six months on a work related assignment at their headquarter during which time she picked up some communicative Chinese and also made the best use of the opportunities available for her to immerse in the Chinese culture.

Migration to the US

Almost a year after Sameera's return to India, Infomatrix asked Sanjay to get ready for a two year long overseas assignment in the US, for one of its clients located in California. The company would take care of the expatriation expenses for the entire family and given family commitments Sameera had to resign her job at Kawavi and move on with Sanjay. Despite a hike in salary, with a family of three, including their newborn baby of eight months, Sanjay was finding it tough to make both ends meet. Sameera had no choice but to search for a job. While the L2 visa with which she landed in the US would allow her to work for any employer as long as Sanjay could work in the US, given the recessionary trends that hit the economy, it was a really tough time to find a job. But, to everyone's surprise, Sameera's qualifications helped played wonders.

Chinese Exposure Helps Sameera

Her experience with Kawavi and her exposure to the Chinese culture, in addition to her origins in India, were things many companies that had Asian tie-ups found really appealing. Soon she landed upon her next job as a tech support engineer for a major video game developer based in the Silicon Valley. This company would prepare the idea blueprints for video games whereas the actual coding and development of the game with consoles would be done by some of the outsourcing companies located in India and China. In general, the hardware was manufactured in China and the software was developed in India. She excelled as an interface between the Indian and the Chinese groups, and connecting both with the Headquarter in the US. Soon, her senior managers found in her promise as a key manager of their overseas operations.

Sameera Filling the Education Deficit

What she lacked was a basic formal training in business. In order to overcome this deficiency, the company sent her to a respected Ivy B-School for multiple short term executive development courses and all her bills were footed by the company. Seeing her enthusiasm, the company managed to arrange for her an H1 visa which would permit her to continue to work for the company irrespective of Sanjay's visa status. And, it turned out that this was timely: due to disruptions in the award of contracts, Infomatrix just recalled Sanjay to go back and rejoin its Bangalore operations.

Sanjay's Re-Education Plunge

Now that Sameera was doing exceedingly well in her career, they both decided that Sanjay quit his job. Sanjay could continue to stay in the US as a dependent of Sameera, on H4 visa class. This visa class would not permit Sanjay to be in the workforce and he decided to make the best use of time by enrolling himself in a university near where they stay, for its MS in computer science program. He studied hard and was awarded the degree in just one year. Given his prior work experience in Infomatrix, he also became one of the first to be selected for a job via on-campus placement. The recruiter also sponsored him for an H1 work visa.

Sanjay Back on the Job

It was no mere coincidence that GPB, his new employer, a major oil and natural gas explorer, have had Infomatrix as one of its outsourcing partners. Sanjay, after undergoing a month long intensive training, that included drilling system programming and survival skills under extreme conditions, is now on a trip to Nigeria where GPB is soon going to be commissioning an oil well. There, he will work with a team of GPB engineers and technicians, sourced from various countries that GPB has operations, with various levels of expertise, to perform the final inspection of the system before its launch.

Career Tweaking Continues

In the meantime, Sameera plans to apply for a business license that would enable her to launch a part-time business in her and Sanjay's name. She believes that their partnership could offer value added consulting for tech businesses in the North America than want to connect with Asian partners and vice versa. Sanjay's parents, both retired from work back home in India, recently came to the US to take care of their newborn baby when Sanjay and Sameera would be busy building their careers.

What Could we Learn from Sanjay and Sameera?

With globalization, there is an increasingly felt need for a globally adaptable workforce that can meet not only the shifting nature of work roles but also the differing expectations of a global mix of stakeholders. As some sectors of the global economy grow at the expense of others and some regions of the world grow faster, unemployment patterns will follow the suit. Become cross-culturally and cross-sectorally adaptive is the way to deal with this.

The case of Sanjay and Sameera highlights the triumph of cross cultural, cross sectoral, adaptiveness. What we see throughout is that this couple overcome hurdles through planned actions and opportunistic behavior. They constantly learned adaptive skills, from the classroom and from the field, and actively sought for opportunities to leverage such skills. It was a challenge for them to adjust themselves to new cultural environments, but their proactive and positive attitude helped them to see opportunities in every new challenging situation. They did not have to knock doors of the publicly or organizationally funded employee support systems; if at all anything helped them, probably it was only the support they received from their families.

The question now is, with Sanjay and Sameera carrying on with their newly found individual career ambitions, how would they still find opportunities for nurturing those family values that originally helped them to reach up to this level.

Academic Career: A Path of No Return?

A couple of weeks back, I got interviewed for the position of the Director of Consumer Insights of a somewhat well-known national retail chain (probably based on the strength of some references). My subjective assessment soon after the one hour long interview held online was that I did an excellent job of presenting myself as a credible candidate for the position. However, I got the feedback yesterday morning that they were no longer considering me for the said position. This made me retrace the entire episode.

Why is an academic professional, fairly well-versed in the marketing literature and successfully published, not seen as a good fit for the position of a consumer research focused job in the industry? You may substitute 'marketing' with any other professional area and ask the same question for seeking the fitness for a corresponding industry position. You may also substitute the word 'professor' with something like PhD / research degree holder.

Was I under-qualified (just because I was over-qualified)? A high school diploma is about what is necessary for a bank teller's job but an MBA is expected these days anyways. How does 'credential creep' (the term for employers demanding unnecessarily more education for every job) not apply beyond a master's degree? Does the industry believe that acquiring a PhD degree and serving some years as a professor or postdoctoral researcher somehow corrodes all the beneficial effects of higher education? A primary school teacher friend of mine, in her sheer humbleness, calls herself a "glorified baby sitter". Are college professors adult sitters? Worse, are academic researchers impractical, pedantic, idea sitters?

These were some of the questions that flashed through my mind soon after I got the rejection letter. Many of my academic colleagues will agree that an academic career is almost always a path of no return (may be, except in extremely research oriented professional fields like the pharmaceutical R&D). It is more or less like joining the order of the Catholic church as a priest: you may give marital counselling, but cannot marry and rear a family. This also explains why many management professors end up as business consultants or even as chubby 'CEO Coaches', but rarely as responsible middle or senior level managers. We are ideally suited at best as dispensable advice churning machines.

In any case, I started a deep conversation on this with some of my old students who are currently in senior recruiter positions. I asked them why they would not prefer PhDs for various jobs. Given below are a sample of their responses (Paraphrased by me):

"PhDs do have skills; but, familiarity with administrative and office procedures is essential for most jobs. In order for such hands-on familiarity, one should work upward through the organizational ladder; a postgraduate school experience cannot substitute that requirement".

"PhDs see the depth of a problem; but, they have a poor grasp of its breadth. Also, they tend to overlook aspects of the problem that are not measurable".

"Academic brains seek to see any new practice by default as the manifestation of an existing theory. One, single, theory. They can't suspend judgment and live a day with multiple possibilities. On the contrary, if you ask a successful businessman, you cannot but notice his comfort level in explaining a situation with multiple, not necessarily compatible, working models".

"PhDs generally have high ego; the ego factor increases in accordance with the number of years you are on a professorship. You are so accustomed to being called sir and madam that you expect it from everyone else in the office. Your subordinates are not your students and your superior is not just a senior professor".

So, what could I say? Do I find merit in these comments? Yes I do, to some extent. Actually, that is one way I reconciled myself with the fact that I was not offered the position for which I was interviewed. I do not wish to find in my higher ed credentials a sweeping excuse for all my various other inadequacies, due to which I might have been deemed unfit for particular jobs, including the one referred above (could be incidentally, during this interview, I was specifically asked "why you choose to work for us after gaining a PhD").

That said, generally speaking, (in my obviously biased) judgment, the concerns about recruiting 'academically overqualified individuals' are over-inflated. They may be carrying with them a set of undesirable thought processes, attitudinal issues, and behavioral patterns primarily stemming from the particularities of their education. But, their intention to join the industry is reason enough to believe that they will take effort to overcome these undesirable elements. Developmental programs aimed at them should just focus on making them mindful of these inadequacies that they might bring into the situation.

In any case, I am of the view that the undesirability weighs far less compared to the value addition they could bring to work. And, lack of familiarity with the 'routines of practice' for most jobs is something that can be overcome in the span of the couple of weeks of 'on the job training'. We live in an increasingly information powered and knowledge driven economy. There is no reason anymore to keep the knowledge producers to within the four walls of academic institutions

Seasons of my Soul

and research laboratories

Why do we (Secretly) Crave for Disasters? The Underpinnings of Thana-Capitalism

Believe it or not, as a culture, we subconsciously crave to hear news about disasters. The magnitude of destruction gives us a curious sense of contentment. In a joint research project with Maximiliano Korstanje, we hypothesize that this has a lot to do with cultural Darwinism.

Based on prior experiences of dealing with doomsdays, a culture would have developed some kind of agility which gets encoded in the genetic traits of that culture. Continued non-use means that it faces the risk of extinction. This will make that culture extremely vulnerable when a great calamity hits it unexpectedly. So, keeping the cultural genes associated with disasters is critically important for the survival of a culture.

Fundamentally, it is this fascination with disasters that has given birth to the phenomenon of 'thana-capitalism'. Cultural expressions that keep the thana genes alive also include imagined disasters depicted in our various contemporary cultural forms. Also, there is no dearth of consumer products that exploit our anxieties about disasters. While none of us want disasters to hit us individually, keeping alive a sense of death and destruction by liminally going through them is the way our cultures have found to deal with disasters.

What Could Successful Marriages Teach us about Employee Retention

Marriage as an institution might be at the declining end of its lifecycle, but there is no limit to what marriages can teach us. Every married person will admit that marriage made them wiser (or, at least, how dumb they were before marriage!). Some of the learnings from the hard feat of maintaining a successful marriage relation can be ported to organizational situations related to employee retention, too.

Various studies give figures anywhere between 50%-200% of the annual salary as the tangible organizational cost of replacing a good employee. The intangible costs like new employee performance issues and damaged reputation as a caring employer are often huge, too. In marital kind of relationship, partners stick together or separate away for reasons other than financial costs or benefits. Thus, drawing parallels between marriage and employee retention is especially useful in understanding how to retain employees when you cannot meet all their financial expectations. Let us see some of these parallels below:

Make clear, what to expect and what is expected, early on. Some premarital dating and courting will help. While dating, don't pretend to be someone else. Understand your potential employee as much as possible during the interviews. Understand unbridgeable differences and don't let them in if such differences are significant enough. Training and development costs will add to the separation cost if they join and then leave after a while. Needless to talk about the burden of emotional infliction.

Immerse them deeply in your culture. Teach them in the vision and mission of the organization beginning from day one. Don't use pamphlets and print manuals to feed them with company information. Tell them stories of organizational valor. For training, use more qualitatively enriching methodologies like case studies. Let them learn while having fun.

Keep mother-in-laws at bay. Mother-in-laws have historically done the commendable job of making familial adjustments rougher and tougher. If possible, identify existing employees having a MIL attitude and keep them away from new employees. However, oftentimes, MIL could be the boss of someone whose subordinate the new employee is. Mother in laws cannot be rooted out and the only reasonable expectation is to treat the MIL disease with proper preparation and counselling.

Be less control oriented and more care oriented. Control is important but controlling is dangerous in relationships. How can you control without being felt as controlling? You care them, show them concern, and fill them with adoration. Let them know how important they are for you. Promise them they are safe in your hands. You will see them singing to your tunes. If in doubt, ask successfully married people. Why would they need more freedom if being chained is the path they would choose irrespective of their available degree of freedom!

Let them foster identities outside of employment. Numerous studies highlight how occasionally staying away makes marriages warmer and stronger. In our times, most of us live a substantial portion of our lives within the boundaries of business organizations. Our personal identities are defined by our organizational affiliations. Increasingly, employees are realizing that their one and only life is too precious to be tied to the singular organizational focus. They crave for attachments and affiliations outside. Encourage them to extend their selves to the communities around. Let them anchor themselves in multiple spots and see the results in performance effectiveness, both individual and organizational. Slavery increases efficiency, freedom improves effectiveness.

Let them co-breed babies with your company. Yes, encourage your employees to spend time on a few side projects the outcome of which they would feel as their own. Officially take the paternity of such outcomes with the organization's label and celebrate. Families with children born to the spouses are more likely to stay together. Let them procreate as many children as possible, rear these children, as long as they meet most other business expectations. Also, you never know some of these children could become your stars!

Don't flirt with candidates perceived as potential replacements. Infidelity is the number one cause of divorces. Sometimes, as managers, you are too tempted to look over the shoulders of your subordinates to find that little younger, little more energetic, employee working in the other division. Sometimes, you are a little unhappy with your subordinate; or, sometimes, you have a deep rooted fear that he or she might ditch you without giving ample notice. As a result, you solicit responses from internal and external candidates by means of a vacant position advertisement. Imagine your wife seeing your profile on a dating or matrimonial website.

Develop synergies that are hard to replicate outside the current business set up. There are certain things you can make your employees exceptionally good at. They should be well known for those unique few things. But, if possible, ensure that they cannot effectively exercise such unique expertise once they decouple themselves from the company. It is not unusual that cohabiting couples develop certain skills and they will continue to stick together just because each of them realizes that the skill is built on the synergy of their partnership.

Communicate honestly and openly, using the right words and tone, at the right time. Adopt a positive psychology approach. Happy couples communicate differently. Let communications to employees exude empathy but also reflect situational nuances. That's what you do when your partner asks you why you went to the game with a colleague of the opposite gender. Let every communicator be trained to read the message they draft from the viewpoint of its receptionist before they hit the send button. Mirroring will help you improve this skill. Use constructive language, wherever possible: Say "you made great coffee yesterday" than to say "today's coffee was not as good" than to say "you made some unsavory coffee today".

Employ silence to silence employees. Communication is vital. But, don't be combative and don't yell at your wife. In many situations, silence serves better than violence. Sometimes, in order to solve a problem, it is best to leave a problem as it is until it dissolves. A lot of discomforting issues in work life are not earth shattering, but they will inflate and explode if we discuss and debate them too much. Married couples know this simple recipe more than any others. Divorces rarely happen over a million dollar housing loan that a spouse has taken without consulting the partner.

Create a healthy extended family environment surrounding work. Frequent community gatherings celebrating business achievements and cultural occasions are vital. Take the employees out on excursions and have honeymoons. Also, important are various opportunities for employees to support each other. These opportunities will help build coping skills, shared beliefs, and an 'at-home-ness' feeling in every employee.

Not staying together is a choice that happy couples don't exercise. The longer an employee gets on with a company, the less likely he will exercise that choice. The initial few days are critical, the initial few weeks are important, but then things will settle down as long as you keep giving them that "little extra" once in a while.

Living a Fulfilled Life beyond the Success-Failure Trap

The Success-Failure Trap

Most so-called motivational gurus pitch for success or suggest that failures are stepping stones to success. They are pauperized in their imaginations. These self-professed experts do some additional damage by programming your minds with their own skewed definitions of success, which unfortunately also transforms you into your own success judges. Alas, once that happens, you have no easy escape from the success-as-objective tangle. The truth is, you don't need to give an iota of care to those irritating people who wait on your way with judgmental swords coated with their colored definitions of success. In the following sections, we will see why.

Life is a Transient State of the Nonliving Matter

Life is a human construct. Life is just a different form of matter. If you wouldn't retort that 'complex' itself is a human construct, I might state that life is just a little more complex (and transient) form of matter than what constitutes nonliving materials. In any case, there is no vacuum between the most advanced life forms and the most primitive nonliving forms. There is a continuum of life in between these extremes of simplicity and complexity.

What if Life is a Degraded Form of the Nonliving Matter?

What if growing into the complex forms is not an up-gradation but rather a degradation? For a moment, look at the profound pristineness and serenity of the mountains and the waters. Then, see the same, in a little degraded version, in the plants. The degradation becomes more visible when we look at the animal life, including that of the man. In some sense, it is a self-serving logic that life is superior to nonlife and it is an illusion that complexity is progress. For the nonliving forms, there is no life nor death. They are not constrained like living forms and nonliving is the purest form of freedom. But, there is a downside, too. The nonliving forms cannot experience that ultimate sense of freedom, that deep peace, that they are so profoundly gifted with. That takes a body, brain, and heart.

The Purpose of the Living Form

Is this an opportunity for us? Yes, indeed it is! Nonliving forms have evolved into living forms so that the former can experience for themselves all the aforesaid blessings. We are nonliving forms boarded on a short tour called life to so that we can experience some of these great values. This is the only true meaning of life, neither successes nor failures defined in terms of material possessions. Put in another way, our success is to be determined based only on whether we have dedicated our lives to experience the greatest values of our nonliving existence, from which we came here and to which we depart.

An Ethical Framework for the Right Conduct

The lure upon us to define success in life in terms of our ability to garner material possessions is a trap. To moderate, material possessions could be pursued only to the extent that they aid us in improving the quality of our nonliving experience. Even then, those material possessions themselves should not determine the success of our lives but rather how such possessions have been deployed in order to experience our nonliving existence. This framework gives us a basis for ethical judgment in that it helps us answer what kinds of material objectives we should pursue.

The Importance of Sharing Material Possessions

Sharing the material possessions becomes a natural consequence once we internalize the above truth. There is no multiplicity of identities among the nonliving forms and if we are the consequence of the urge of the nonliving matter to experience the value of its existence, it makes perfect sense to mutually endow as many other living forms as possible to experience it. Such sharing also helps us to experience the unity of our nonliving reality. It is only when such sharing takes place life forms attain the pinnacle of glory.

One Person's Failure is Our Collective Failure

If you think further through this framework, it is not hard to realize that your failure is not actually your failure: it is rather the collective failure of everyone else to nurture you, as a result of which our collective nonliving essence did not get a chance to experience its beauty through your body.

In Summary

Live your life, measure it not with the successes associated with gaining material artifacts. Life is becomes valuable only through the life-transcending experiences of the living body. This thought, if internalized, can liberate you from the peripheries of a limiting life defined in terms of successes and failures.

When Freshness Triumphs over Work Experience

First, this is not a discussion about the value of a college degree (our cultural default is to equate lack of work experience with holding a college degree!). I have the faintest of intention to join the debate on why college dropouts like Bill Gates and Steve Jobs are more successful than most doctoral degree holders in computer engineering. My objective is only to help recruiters rethink the pivotal importance, across the board, they attribute to work experience while they consider someone for a job.

By eliminating freshers from the search process, employers might be undervaluing some of the key benefits of lack of work experience and simultaneously overrating the paybacks of work experience. Let me highlight some of the often neglected costs of experience:

Freshness is inversely proportionate to experience. Experience in many professions is synonymous with 'future-blind' just as much as it is with 'past-proof'. At their best, they will be the custodians of the 'best practices'. But, remember, competitive advantage comes with (creative) destruction and not by preserving the past order. If you are looking for out of the box ideas, look unto the unpolluted rebellious mind of a fresher.

Experienced employees may have preset for themselves a career path. Experienced employees who accept the current job are also more likely to have set for themselves a career trajectory (and ambitions!) – for their next two or three jobs, at least. If a company plans to mend them for something else in the future, you can expect them revolting, vitiating the work environment, and possibly leaving the company.

You often pay the experienced ones a high premium for starting on day 1 as if it were day 31. Many jobs don't have a steep and arduous learning curve making it not so vital to have tremendously experienced people occupying them. Why would you hire a five year experienced cashier in a bank for a 25% extra pay! Likewise, experience statements hide more than what they reveal: If you want your admin assistant to know Mac OS don't recruit someone with fifteen years of entrenched experience in Operating System use. Never know she may be experienced in the use of MS Windows! Unlearning is harder than learning.

Why are the experienced folks here if their experience was valuable there? This is a Socratic question that might reveal a lot of mud. If they had a celebrated work history elsewhere for the same or a similar job, why should they be leaving all that and joining hands with you! May be they were not really valuable there? They had attitudinal issues, if not task performance issues? Well, I don't deny there could be very genuine reasons for seeking a move.

In many cases, prior experiences are only minimally related to the present job requirements. It is not bad to hire a ten year experienced doctor as a hospital director. But, how closely related is the experience as a physician for the position of a hospital administrator? Likewise, why would you prefer a fifteen year experienced retired pilot as your chauffeur?

Experienced employees continue to work at their old jobs in the new workplace. Everyone knows why Google won't recruit a Microsoft employee or why Toyota won't recruit a Ford employee. How often do you hear someone talking about the good times he had at the previous workplace (that he left happily!). They have such poor adaptability to the new organizational culture, multiple studies show. More on this to follow.

Experienced employees might need equal or more mentoring. Sure they know 'the task at hand'. But, what if they don't find the same socio-technical systems integrating the job with the overall workplace and beyond? Loss of personal meaning is something certain to follow. Experienced employees first should mentally decouple themselves from the task environment they are familiar with before they could (try to) engage meaningfully with the new environment. Here, mentors have the additional headache of knowing how the prior work environment for the newly recruited experienced employee was.
Experience hides situational success factors: Say, Jim is an experienced investment banker. But how much of the return on investment that he brought in was the result of the 'lucky times' he was there in the industry?

Experience is more about the bones and much less about the meat. Yes, he wants to become a dean because he was a professor for ten years. Experience orientation highlights chronology but neglects some of the important qualifications to become a dean, like wider stakeholder relations.

Yes, work experience does have its pros: among other things, it is often a litmus test of one's interest in their field of work and it might provide a quite valid proof of one's ability to do things. There is virtually no job posting that says "you will not be considered if you have some relevant work experience". That said, as you have seen above, downsides are galore in having work experience as your only yardstick.

I do not wish to abandon the importance of work experience: say, you would not give someone a job as a pilot just because he is inspired. The 'ideal' situation is to keep an attitude of freshness in mind and creative imagination along with a track record of learning enriching work experience. Most often, experience takes away the freshness and that should ring the alarm bells.

So, will I have a fresher or an experienced person as the CEO? A fresher for sure, if it is a small tech start up. Otherwise, it depends.

Strategic Paralysis in Network Organizations

Theodore Levitt earned a legacy by introducing the term "marketing myopia" and detailing how organizations fail by being short-sighted. Gurus are supposedly strategic thinkers and it is understandable that they are fascinated about the visions at the end of the tunnel.

The opposite of myopia is hyperopia: in medical terms, it is a vision condition in which distant objects can be seen clearly, but close ones do not come into proper focus. In business philosophy, hyperopia is not trendy and did not receive any significant attention: however, nature doesn't exempt anyone, even those occupying the CEO gowns, from the need to make (or, at least oversea) some decisions affecting the next moment. A lot of business failures happen not because of the lack of long term vision, but by the sheer neglect of seemingly trivial issues right ahead.

Hierarchy is one of the worst enemies of innovation and contemporary design thinkers abhor it. Network organizations are rightly praised for the same reason. Yet, traditional organizations that are structured hierarchically have an inbuilt design feature which allocate strategic, tactical, and operational decisions and resources across the hierarchy. This prevented lower management from strategizing and disincentivised higher management from nitpicking upon day to day operations.

A central problem with the network structure is that strategy has become everyone's cup of coffee. The expression *analysis paralysis* is well known: it refers to how over-thinking might lead to under-action. In network organizations, something akin to this happens with regard to strategy. Because of the flatness of structure, strategy has become pan-organizationally pervasive.

Of course, attention to daily operations too could have become so. But, given the choice to strategize (a.k.a. do armchair thinking) or to dirty one's feet in the muddy road right ahead, human preferences are obvious. Based on my interactions with management consultants and my own consulting experiences in network organizations, I would state that the time an average employee spends on matters traditionally considered strategic is disproportionately high. Long range thinking is awesome - except for our scarcity of time. Yet, it takes attention away from the survival needs of the present and more importantly the need for building from bottom up to grab the dreams.

How to overcome strategic paralysis while exploiting all the advantages of the network structure? Let me end this note with this open-ended question.

Why Businessmen should Treat Business Professors better

First, 'Hate' is a hugely exaggerated word and it should not be there in the title of this article. The only reason for it to be there is to increase marketability. That said, the rest of the article is not really market-oriented and may very well be perceived as overly apologetic.

Okay, I am a business professor, with a PhD in Management and more than a decade of experience in higher education. I spent most of my career thus far as a true-to-the-spirit theorist, but (tried to) engage with the practicing community as often as I could. Very often, one reverential feedback that I get from my former MBA students is that "what we do now is very different from what we learned in the classroom". Well, I knew they were respectful enough to use the word 'different' in the place of something like 'absolute bullshit' and 'what we learned' in the place of 'what you taught'. I do agree that some of what business professors teach is overcooked esoteric philosophy packaged as wisdom and I confess that I partake in it for a living, too. One lingering perception the practitioners have about us career academicians is that they consider us as contributing nothing valuable. Ironically, that perception reaches its peak when the practitioners are MBA graduates themselves, taught by some of the theoretically brightest minds while they were students a while back.

More ironically practitioners do embrace a vulgarized version of academic wisdom when they open up their doors for management gurus – most of them without any real business experience or even without a PhD - who offer consulting services. According to Matthew Stewart, the Oxford trained philosopher turned management consultant, beginning with the foundational works of F.W. Taylor, the history of management consulting is full of shams. He cites sources to indicate that Taylor fudged data to prove the merits of his so-called 'scientific management' and then charged businesses hefty sums as consulting fee. Even for me, it is hard as hell to understand why practicing managers with decades of experience managing successful companies blindly trust the glorified wisdom of outside consultants (again, I must confess that I too am a - fairly unsuccessful - consultant).

While not disagreeing with the naysayers entirely, my attempt here is to reason the benefits of business practitioners learning from business theorists like me. I must clarify that I am not advocating that you consider taking up an MBA degree from a flashy league school that would make you go financially broke for the next 20-30 years of your life. With that caveat, let me list my arguments out:

The theoretical orientation that we provide helps businessmen to see the bigger picture beyond their current business. Yes, many 'uneducated' managers and entrepreneurs suffer from an acute shortsighted vision that the singular foundation and outcome of business both are profits and that everything else is a nuisance. We teach them to see the broader socio-cultural-economic-technologic fabric within the perimeters of which businesses work and how creatively engaging with these environments determine the success of businesses. Yes, if you can learn all these yourself without the framework of a formal curriculum that we offer, that's awesome. But, that is easier said than done.

Businessmen may be action heroes, but we prepare them to become thought leaders as well. I do not claim that all b-school professors do this equally. But, the time spent with a theory minded professor is like experimenting in a laboratory setting where you could experiment without really harming the real world. Yes, as someone pointed out, classrooms are laboratories where potential futures keep brewing. Not everything that you reflect upon need not be implemented in practice: but, it is not a bad idea to think through multiple alternatives and choose the best one out of them for implementation. Learning comes from reflective doing. A professor with a PhD will help you perfect that art of reflective doing. Some commentators have suggested that you should complete a classical theory oriented degree program like Economics, Sociology, or Psychology, rather than an MBA, because "business is all about understanding patterns from the history of mind – of individual and of the society". While the above statement is true, the progress of mind is characterized by 'emergence' of the new in creative ways and classical disciples are very conservative in admitting this creative emergence. In comparison with the professors of discipline oriented studies like Economics, who teach students to see the future solely based on history, we business professors have a trans-disciplinary orientation and we are significantly more open to creative reflections. This will help students to deal better with innovative business opportunities in new business environments.

Our focus is to make your knowledge portable. Not just more knowledge, but also more clarity about the relatedness of knowledge in various realms. Okay, you have succeeded with your business in an industry. You have developed a lot of sector specific insights. But, porting all that to other industries or even to other national cultural contexts is not easy. Imagine you want to get into other markets or industries as part of your growth process as a businessman. Good business professors will help you see your plant as a tree in the forest. In other words, a holistic perspective spanning the entire business world. Also, while on campus, remember to engage in a philosophical discussion with your professors about your career choices and their personal meaning.

We are cross-trained experts who can teach you a plethora of skills. What we teach you is not only armchair philosophy. We can teach you some accounting (what you will learn from an Accounting program), some forecasting (what you will learn from an Economics program), some human behavior (what you would learn from a Psychology program), some data analysis (what you will learn from a Statistics program), some information technology (what you will learn from a Computer Science program), some writing skills (that you would learn from a Language / Literature / Journalism program), etc. Good business school professors are a 'jack of all trades', in a good way. More importantly, we can mentor the students to fuse the apparently unrelated skills together to make synergies. If you don't believe, ask engineers who 'grew into' managerial roles without any b-school training how hard their transition was.

We are a breed of positive philosophers but we can as well be harshly analytical-reductionistic devil's advocates. We are protected from the consequences of our advices and we don't have to die for our faiths, thanks to what we call our academic freedom. We can wear multiple, often mutually incompatible, hats to attack an issue at hand. While all that can seem impractical and a waste of time, being able to dissect and re-merge the pieces related to an issue are sure help you sometime down the lane. And, we give you that orientation and training.

Note that I have (quite deliberately) avoided some benefits of attending a b-school, like networking opportunities, perceived prestige, perceived credibility, etc., from this list. While such items are important, there are easier alternatives to achieve these and that we professors do not contribute much in terms of students gaining them. In the ultimate analysis, the key value that we add to your life is what Plato said long back: liberate the prisoners from the world of their immediate sensations, lead them to experience the more fundamental world of ideas.

A final word of advice to MBA aspirants: Don't go to a b-school predominantly packed with the academically disinclined clinical professors of practice who are advertised to be 'industry-oriented'. If your objective is to learn practice, just don't come to a business school. A better and more cost-effective option is to join as an apprentice / intern in a business house.

The Positive Revolution in Tourism Studies

Studies after studies show that there are certain emotional states that engage with the body on the one side (the 'pleasure principle', creating pleasure) and the spirit on the other side (the 'meaning principle', creating meaning). Attuning us to such emotional states is probably the clue to a healthy life and, beyond all, our true happiness.

What are the means available for us to attain those emotional states? Tourism could be an important one. It is worth exploring if and how tourism can contribute to the generation and nurturing of the aforesaid emotional states. Unfortunately, tourism has thus far been treated just like many other interventions that are aimed at reducing negativity rather than celebrating positivity. Even the most mainstream definition of tourism itself is that it is a temporary escape from the malady of routinized monotonous work life and that the transformations borne out of tourism are merely liminal.

The fact: tourism had never been about survival necessity. The psychological principles developed to understand survival challenges are extremely ill-suited to understand tourism. Yet, dominant tourism literature does exactly the same thing - call upon such principles to explain the whole gamut of tourism phenomenon. When such explanations are translated into marketing practice, the underlying assumption is that of a pathetic human existence that would do good by means of a little bit of transient 'fooling around'. Tourism as a tool in the neo-Freudian pathology! Theory and marketing practice are hand in gloves together in downplaying the life changing effects of travel.

Tourism is a very dynamic phenomenon indeed. The dynamism is often reflective of the underlying changes in the society. Sometimes, tourism partners with such changes; sometimes, tourism resists such changes; sometimes, tourism creates such changes. Just as we say 'change is the only constant', there is some constancy, a deeper sense of un-change-ability, a common strand, that would interconnect all kinds of touristic pursuits, held at all phases in history and geography. The human search for positive life changing experiences is that common denominator. It is high time we recognize tourism as a positive force celebrating human emancipation rather than as a temporary suppressant of otherwise negative lives.

Tourism is not an end in itself, but rather a pathway for the seekers of good life. Imagine if the industry scripted tourism around positive life changing experiences. Imagine if the quality of service provided to tourists was measured based on whether the service exceed expectations about positive experiences (Or, better, based on whether the services help tourists create these experiences in personally meaningful ways). Imagine if tourism researchers had examined how tourism products, organizations, and business environments have evolved as a response to the underlying need to revel in enlightened life experiences.

Bernie Sanders and the "Frankenstein Monster Problem in Leadership"

Bernie Sanders, the campaigner for the US Democratic presidential nomination 2016, raises an interesting leadership problem. The curious case of Bernie shows that 'leadership as an ideal' can take on a life of its own, even if the 'leader as a person' who originally personified the ideal backtracks. Indications are that Bernie absolutely lost control of the political upheaval that he inaugurated with his bid for candidacy.

The mood of those who continue to 'feel the bern' is that the person by name Bernie Sanders does not matter anymore. It was as though people were looking for an initial thrust for the mechanics of the movement to get into the mode of self-sustenance: Bernie provided that thrust and now it did not matter if he was there to nurture it.

Historically, most revolutions that lost the support of their founding leaders have gone into disarray and eventually faltered off. Or, some exogenous forces will capitalize upon them and give new spins, before that happens. Will the master strategist Trump capture upon this tremendous momentum that is now devoid of personified direction? I see some symbolism of the Pied Piper of Hamelin in him. Will he take away the Berie herd? I wouldn't want to speculate or take a side. Also, I am not a voter nor a supporter of any political faction in this fray. This note is just meant to be a pedantic observation.

Celebrating Imagination

To imagine is to become naturally human. The blessing of imagination is not granted to every species and man is truly privileged. Yet, imagination is often despised and society demonizes it. The unimaginativeness of the custodians of societal order tend to see imagination as the antonym of reason.

However, every idea that stands to reason now has a history and most likely a future. This 'imaginative continuum' of ideas implies that our worthwhile ideas are all products of persistent human enterprise, our openness to embrace 'facts-in-the making'. Reason is the body and imagination is the spirit that propels it.

Below, I summarize the methodologies of my strivings for an imagination-filled life:

Allow the content and direction of your imaginative experiences a free flow. Whenever possible, unwind your mind, remove the traffic rules for ideas, and let the ideas dance together with no control whatsoever. Observe formations and emergence of new groupings of ideas without a judgmental frame. Tip: Keep an alarm for one hour for you to return to the routine existence.

If you find yourself under the grip of imagination and if you become aware of it, let that awareness not impact the ongoing presence of imagination. But, just be aware and observe the process.
At times, it is good to strain for imagination. But, restrict that to situations where the imaginative urge asks you to do so. Going up to the mountain cliff to glide down is a good metaphor: predictably generate enough potential energy to later transform it into the free flow kinetic energy of ideas.

Do not limit your imaginations to 'practical' topics. You never know, imagining about angels may help you better solve a practical problem like flying. But, that's not the matter: imagination in itself is worthwhile! Your purpose in life is to celebrate your life and what celebration is without some raw imagination! Just learn to love fantasies for what they are (not) worth!

Our collective systems are geared for measuring fulfilled potential; their algorithms are designed to reward the achievement of predicted outcomes. This unitary orientation, doesn't reward the human urge to release potentials of newer kinds. Yes, rewarding for outcomes before the outcomes themselves are available is reckless and it is understandable why societies are hesitant to pay for them, especially when the seekers employ so far untested methodologies. But, at an individual level, such fears should have very little room: my advice is that you spend just enough time and effort upon activities that fetch you your daily bread and then dedicate the rest of your life for imaginative pursuits that help define for yourself who you are!

I want to start afresh,

I wish to bid adieu,

Every experience, good or bad,

This game lost its sheen.

I want to start afresh,

A bright new game,

With new rules, tools, and mates,

This game lost its sheen.

Organizational Complexity is NOT Disorder

Complexity is not disorder and increase in complexity is not increase in entropy. However, if you look narrowly, you may confuse between the two.

A good (and simple) example: currently in your organization, you have one subordinate, one direct superior, and one at-your-level coworker. Imagine that this is changed - say, as a result of formal organizational restructuring or as employees 'violating' the set norms due to the increased opportunities for 'social networking'. To the one looking only at the tree and not the forest (a.k.a. the ultra-reductionist), this is chaotic: too many communication lines, zigzag interactions, and too much information to deal with. He would lament that the organization is running down.

It might take a long while before he realize that what he perceived as mayhem was actually delivering better results for the organization: better solutions, more innovations, and increased stakeholder approval for decisions. In other words, the perceived disorder was an increase in some kind of deeper order. Complexity is not disorder but a higher order order.

It is not my view that you can increase orderliness in an organization by means of introducing complexity. My argument is just that increasing complexity often has the effect of a 'quantum leap' in the orderliness and not a linear or continuous increase. Technology has done that in many organizations, wonderfully.

Now, the most important point: if, in case, an increase in complexity does not cause such a discontinuous jump in orderliness (or, does not result in a qualitatively different orderliness of a different mode), it is deadly and will prove the reductionist right. Increasing complexity that does not change mode is increase in entropy: it will cause to run down the organization and will kill the organizational system sooner than later.

In summary, within each mode of complexity, there is an acceptable minimum and maximum level of (dis)order. The vibrancy of an organizational system is evidenced by whether it is responding to the natural, universal, process of entropy by means of leapfrogging into a deeper level of more complex, more agile, order.

Are Myths 'Real'? My Meditations on the Cultural Logic of Myths

For quite some time, I had been meditating over myths. Yes, myths are real. Just as real as the dynamics of the society in which you live in: as real as its power relations, level of discontent, its aspirations, etc.

Let me try to make things simple.

Myths encase the aspirations of a society. Remember, a society is equally what is aspires to be as what it actually is. What a society aspires to be is often just a simple transformation of what it actually is. Say if a society has got unjust power relations, what it aspires is its transpose: just power relations. The reality and the aspirations of a society both constitute the dynamics of that society.

When the reality deteriorates or the aspirations exceed, the gap between them increases. Beyond a threshold minimum gap, representative members of a society undergoing this gap are compelled to carve out the prevalent aspirations 'in the form of a reality that existed in the past'. The aspirations carved out this way are the candidates waiting to become the myths of that society. One or only a few out of this set are finally embraced by the collective consciousness of a society (because of their superior representational power) and these become the actual myths of that society. So, myths are real, because these represent the real.

One more issue remains to be answered. I stated in the previous paragraph that myths are carved out in the form of a reality that existed in the past. Why not these myths be expressed just in the form of future possibilities? Here, the answer is straightforward. The objective of a myth is to make the consumer of it to buy its real possibility. When one is told a particular kind of reality existed in the past, it is much easier to make that person to work towards it (because 'it worked in the past' and it can work again!) than when you merely tell that person that the reality expressed in the myth is merely a vision for for a better future that we need to try to build. In other words, the cultural logic behind myths is that, aspirations when expressed as past realities are more effective in guiding societal progress.

"Maintain Eye-Contact" - Interviewers, AVOID demanding it!

After campus interviews, it is common that some of my otherwise bright students come to me lamenting "I could not maintain eye contact". I often hear interview board members lamenting the same: "some of your students are very terrible in maintaining eye contact".

Our collective infatuation with this whole 'eye contact' thing has personally impacted me negatively, throughout my life. I must admit that I am very 'bad' at maintaining eye contact during conversations. It is the natural me and that I have never felt bad about it until one day a friend of mine called me up after an interview that I attended at a semi-prestigious US University for a faculty position to tell me that the interview board members very apprehensive of the fact that I did not maintain eye contact during my research presentation". O what a grave sin I might have committed! After this incident, I read multiple self-help books on eye contact improvement and even attended a short-term paid training. I wouldn't say these did not help me. But, that is not the whole story.

I noticed that an 'improvement' in eye contact almost always led to a decrease in my focus on the content of what I presented. This is no quantum theory: focus on eye contact would increase your 'presentability' (thanks to a stupid cultural norm!); yet, the needs of your brain are neglected in that process. Your brain will feel a stiffness, decapacitation, and an inability to be what it is and to deliver the authentic you, rationally and creatively. In summary, interviewers demanding primal importance to eye contact just don't get to hear the story they should be listening to. How pathetic that we recruit people for their eyes!

My later research led me to find more merits in to the above claim. Among other places, vital evidence comes from psychology: Eye Movement Desensitization and Reprocessing (EMDR) is a therapy used to help victims of trauma to recover from the grips of their painful experiences. The basic idea is that stiffened eyes are associated with viewing the world as a traumatic situation and that de-stiffening eye movements are helpful in finding more meaningful and enriching perspectives. Rapid eye movement (REM) sleep, a natural stage in the sleep even among animals, pretty much achieves the same. It might be an "alluring and sexy" feeling (in the language of a girl student of mine in India who told me that one interviewer asked her to keep looking at his eyes) for the interviewers when interviewees stare at them - but, that fixation defeats the larger purpose.

Remember, eye contact doesn't necessarily mean confidence, interest, or understanding. There is no empirical research linking eye contact with any of its purported benefits. It is just our collective illusion. If you want to test these qualities in your candidates, put them through real situations. Let them move their eyes along with their tongues and cheeks as you interview them!

Relating Effectual Logic with 'Rational Logic'

According to the literature, effectuation is a set of decision-making principles expert entrepreneurs are observed to employ in situations of uncertainty.

I would like to propose a new definition of effectuation based on pre-rationality, rationality, and post-rationality. Before that, let us understand that higher levels of rationalities contain within them all the relatively lower levels of rationalities. Also, it is the middle-range rationality that is appealing to the brain (pre-rationality appeals to the heart; post-rationality appeals to the soul).

In the above background, effectuation may be defined as the process of reducing the post-rational to the rational.

Essentially, this is what all the innovators do. Entrepreneurship is the function of projecting the post-rational upon the rational-material world so that the reflection of it will share the dimensions of the rational. Somewhat like the map-making process. Post-rational reality is sensed by means of 'the mind's eye' and the mind processes and rationalize it at the mid-range rational level.

The reflected image of the post-rational upon the mind will then be compared and contrasted with the current material reality sensed through 'the body's eye' by the entrepreneur. This exercise will give him a material idea of the 'gap' between the two. Innovations - products and services - are those things that materially bridge this gap.

Likewise, we can frame what artists do as the process of reducing the rational to the pre-rational. Thoughts?

'Spirituality Infected' B-Schools

I believe B-schools should increase the scientific temper of students than sell them snake oil packaged as spirituality. Self-professed god men have easier access to B-Schools (until they are jailed!) than free thinkers. Even many well-known business educators have metamorphosed themselves into spiritual management gurus. Yet, recent research shows that merely thinking about science (NOT concocted spirituality) enhances moral behavior of individuals.

See this Scientific American article:

http://www.scientificamerican.com/article.cfm?id=just-thinking-about-science-triggers-moral-behavior

Noticeably, there is equal or more deterioration in the sphere of 'spiritual business' than it is in the 'material business', as evidenced by all the scams and scandals involving god-men and gurus.

In the spirit of the article I cited above, why not we rather increase the scientific temper of our students than sell them the spiritual alternative - especially if moral enrichment is the objective? By the way, I am a great fan of the Talmudic wisdom, the Upanishads, the Bhagvatgita, and the various works of great mystics. Yet, in our roles as business educators-cum-spiritual gurus, we end up doing an exercise of 'far fetching' the messages of these great texts while trying to link them with the world of business.

I just reviewed a book titled 'Bible for Business' and was wondering why the author was struggling so hard to twist and turn scriptures to bring home simple logical viewpoints like "be good to your customers"!

Renewed Hopes for True Globalization: A Silver Lining from Brexit

Two major versions of globalization have been happening for quite some time: one, business interest driven super-nationalism packaged as globalization (eg: "The EU") and two, a more genuine version of globalization inspired by the rising global consciousness of people, aided by the (social-media) technological revolutions. In a way, Brexit is a good sign that the former version might be failing.

Years back during a debate, I took the position that the success of incremental regional integration projects like the Euro Zone will actually thwart the radical project of true global integration. The simple reason for this is that regional blocks are more likely to protect their internal turfs than single nation states. The internal power struggles within such blocks make further radical integration a far cry. Especially, the winners from the project (like the poor countries from Eastern Europe that clearly benefitted from the EU project) do not want any further expansion. Likewise, the losers (like "the British people") who taste the bitterness of smaller integrations become wary of any further incremental integration and may actually want to regress to the traditional nation state model.

Globalization should be guided by a global blueprint from the start and that it should not be the piecemeal integration of regional blocks. I believe it should happen organically than as the bulldozed initiative of a group of countries. I do see some silver lining in the failure of globalization as a transnational business project.

Yes, every cloud has a silver lining. May Brexit reinvigorate our strivings for a more humane and holistic version of global integration.

Why Sustainable Competitive Advantage is a Bad Idea: A (Dis)service to Porter et al.

Sustained competitive advantage in an industry will kill that industry. Competition skews your strategies to those few things that would help you fed off competition, resulting in the neglect of more objectively important priorities. The innate drive to evolve and become better will suffer greatly in cut-throat competition. Once one or a few players in an industry achieves 'sustained competitive superiority', such competitive dynamics leads to the entire industry becoming innovation resistant.

Oftentimes, we see the benefits of competition. We see the benefits, including innovations that competition brings about. Unfortunately, we cannot lab-test the alternative hypothesis: i.e., would innovations have been possible or qualitatively different if the competitive dynamics were different. Well, we do have experiences about industries surrounded by different kinds of business environments and have evidence of how such differences have differently impacted innovativeness within an industry.

From my analysis about various industries, I have arrived at the conclusion that competition is not essential for the beneficial societal effects from an industry as long as the members in that society adheres to certain higher order values. For example, in societies that value them, values expressed in statements such as "by our action today upon what our predecessors had handed over to us yesterday, we will make a better tomorrow" are powerful enough to pulverize our collective energies for doing good. Or, leave that: even among us, haven't we seen numerous individual artists and scientists who perform better and produce far superior outcomes when they work in their own secluded spheres, steering away from the competitive dynamics? If this is true at the individual level, why can't it be true in the organizational or the industry level?

If the above situation is not possible in historically and culturally competition infused societies (a.k.a. western societies), what is important is to ensure that competition does not lead to sustainable competitive advantage for a few (almost impossible!). Lack of sustained competitive advantage will at least give room for players to seek that Holy Grail – left, right, up, down, inward, and outward. But, once a few leading seekers grab that Holy Grail, lo, the industry shifts to a gear of status quo. If at all anything better is to happen, one has to wait until exogenous innovations directed from other industries unsettle that gloomy, dreary, sustenance.
This is heresy and I know the fans of Michael Porter likes will rage in anger to kill me. Or, may be, neglecting is a better option to silence dissent.

Heisenberg on Validity Vs Reliability: The Uncertainty Principle in Quantum Social Reality

Heisenberg's Uncertainty Principle in physics asserts a fundamental limit to the precision with which certain pairs of physical properties of a particle known as complementary variables, such as position and momentum, can be known simultaneously: say, the more precisely the position of a particle is determined, the less precisely its momentum can be known, and vice versa.

When I reflect upon my experience as a social researcher, one thing that often strikes my mind is the difficulty to concurrently get hold of two vital elements of a good measurement system - validity and reliability - without errors. We aim to attain perfect validity and reliability in our measurements: we want that what we measure should be the right thing and that the measurements should be consistent across trials. Social research methodology literature suggests that attaining both of these is fairly simple and straightforward, with the help of diagrams like the one given below:

Unreliable & Unvalid   Unreliable, But Valid

Reliable, Not Valid   Both Reliable & Valid

However, ask a practicing research methodologist. More likely than not, you will find uncertainties and inconclusiveness impinging his reply. Is there a fundamental difficulty in co-grabbing the best values for both validity and reliability? I believe there indeed is. It is just that in some cases (like in the archery diagram given above), the uncertainty tends to zero.

When the degree of complexity of a social reality increases, attempting to obtain consistently stable measurements (reliable measurements) will reduce the chances of our ability to extract the momentum of that social reality (valid measurements) - and vice versa. For me, reliability is akin to the position of a subatomic particle and validity has a deep 'spiritual' semblance with the momentum.

There might be a 'classical social reality' and a 'quantum social reality'. Or, we can take classical measurements or quantum measurements upon a particular social reality. The classical social reality may just be a pragmatic compromise that provides a working model for day to day social life. May be, when you try to measure social reality at the quantum level, there is a minimum constant (K) for the product of the uncertainties of validity (V) and reliability (R) such that $\Delta V \Delta R \geq K$.

George, Babu P.

On Being a Research Practitioner: Some Personal Reflections

While preparing the proposal for PhD admission, my biggest fear was whether I had identified a significant research problem. I knew I did not know a lot about research methods; but I also knew that universities would be relatively lenient about it in the early stages of research. Well, it took for me a couple of months to come up with the current research problem - what if the expert committee vetoed it. I wanted to become a career academic and a PhD was the license to it.

As I feared, the committee did not find my research problem particularly interesting. There were too many negative comments about my methodology, too. My intuition muttered that I would not be selected. I felt very bad: I already knew I was not great at doing industry jobs and now I felt I am not good for an academic career either. It was such an agony that I couldn't sleep well that night. The next day morning, my potential supervisor called me with a good news: I was given tentative admission on condition that I reformulate my research agenda within the next six months. That was more than a life saver!

That evening I went to the library - not to start my literature review, but to check out a few motivational books. I really needed some counsel. However, I am not a person of typical temperament who would be satisfied with the golden verses of religious texts or the ready-to-eat tips of motivational gurus. I find peace, happiness, and inspiration by reading philosophy. Yes, I was driven by my impulses to the philosophy books section in the library. That was a major turning point.

My eyes somehow landed on to a book that fundamentally altered my life. It was none other than Carl Popper's "The Logic of Scientific Discovery". I felt like each word in that book was increasing my hunger, a rare kind of hunger I began to love thence. Overnight, I understood a fundamental problem with the research I had planned for my doctoral dissertation: the hypotheses I had were not falsifiable. I have also learned from this book about a number of issues that have always remained current in research theory. For a while, I felt as if I was drifting away from the issue of identifying a particular tree (my research problem) in order to gain a view of the entire forest (the theory of research). Yes, I indeed was: the next in line for me to feast my thirsty mind was Thomas Kuhn's "The Structure of Scientific Revolutions". After these two books, my curiosity led me to explore how the fundamental issues discussed by Popper and Kuhn would apply to research in humanities and social sciences. In the next couple of months, with the same passion, I read at least half a dozen books on 'research methods' written from diverse ontological and epidemiological premises. For the first time, research for me ceased to be a way to get a PhD and subsequently secure a respectable and decently paid job. Notwithstanding the fact that I still did not have a proper research problem to be presented to the university research committee, I began to feel a deep joy that nurtured my passion - I would call it the 'joy for discovery' - which lives with me even today.

While my readings did not present me with any tailor-made research problems, I was made to realize a very important principle: the world is full of answers waiting to be revealed to the one with the right questions. Yes, everything that you see is an answer to some question. Since these answers are often right in front of your senses, it is a good thing to begin your journey from them - begin by meditating upon the answers, then all the way backward, until you shed light on the right question. For me, this was to be my hands on research strategy, rather than an armchair reflection. I do this all the time and it has helped me tremendously as a researcher.

Oftentimes, we might think that certain questions are evidently solved and that it is worthless to dissect the obvious. The truth is, even when you think a problem is solved, even when you think an area of inquiry is saturated with the right answers, there is still room for further inquiries. That is more to do with the fundamental nature of knowledge itself: knowledge never allows anyone to see herself naked; rather, what the researchers are presented with are (often progressively better) models of knowledge. This fact should be sufficient to humble the most fanatically egotistical researcher. Unfortunately, most upstart crows among us (and many seasoned players, too!) do not understand this. In broader terms, it is important for researchers to have a worldview and it is no less important to be aware of that. According to me, every researcher should have an answer for each of these questions: What are your ontological beliefs? (Do you hold that absolute reality exists?) What are your epistemological beliefs? (Do you hold that reality can be accessed as it is?).

The other side of what I mentioned above is when you become uncomfortable to think along certain lines or to ask certain questions. On the one hand, this process will make you realize your weaknesses and increase self-reflection (very important for a researcher); on the other hand, if you are too uncomfortable about something, the treasure of knowledge might well be there!

I also want to stress about is the pivotal importance of joining the right conversations. It never occurred to me that this was important until I moved to the US where there was micro-specialization for everything. With an ever-increasing number of specializations, it becomes difficult to identify a large pool of scholars sharing the same tastes and preferences. Listservs, e-groups, and web 2.0 social networks help to some extent, but not always. Sometimes, especially if you are someone who pioneer a new research area, you have to take the initiative to gather interested fellow researchers and begin a new conversation. Peer acceptability is an important criterion for success in research and conversations pave the way for it. While the aforesaid is widely known, what is relatively unknown is the beneficial effects of engaging conversations with scholars working on other knowledge fields. The grey areas between disciplines are not well defined and conversations are often difficult because of differing philosophies, principles, and practices. Despite these difficulties, whenever such conversations are effectively held, radical innovations in knowledge ensues. What I advocate by the term conversion is not limited to the networking among like-minded individuals: at times, it turns out to be for the good of everyone if you could 'provoke' a community of researchers by asking uncomfortable questions - so that they can see how naked they are. If you cannot join an ecosystem, challenge it from outside!

At this stage, I want to share with you a really bad experience one of my friends had. She completed a research project and submitted a manuscript reporting the study to a journal. She was extremely careful about not sharing it with anyone. The journal rejected the paper and she decided to improve it before submitting it elsewhere. Among other chores, it took almost six months for her to do the same. In the meantime, a Google search by her presented to her a shocking result: her paper with minimal changes has appeared in an online journal, but with someone else as the author. From where might it have been leaked? She thinks it is from one of the anonymous reviewers. In any case, she worked hard, presented evidences of her authorship (thankfully, she had her submission email to the journal), and made the online journal to remove the manuscript. Recently, I was told that the professor who plagiarized the work did not get any punishment whatsoever. This series of events heighten the importance of one thing: quite contrary to commonsense, you should make your work-in-progress as widely available as possible. Create internet imprints of your works in progress by uploading them on social sites and networks. Let everyone know that you are working on it. The best way to protect your work is to show it to the world (before someone else does it!).

Okay, let me pause for now and respond some of the questions that you might have about research:

Q: As a researcher, is it important for me to always adhere to my belief about the nature of reality and how that reality can be known?

A: Intellectual honesty is very important. People who follow your research are very likely to find out discrepancies if you make them conveniently. However, that does not prevent you from changing your views on the nature and accessibility of reality as long as you report the same in your research reports and as long as you shift from one extreme to the other extreme too many times just for convenience. I know of a fellow researcher who is pragmatic. He does not find any fault with what I said above. According to him, he is free to shift his brain from one worldview to the other keeping in view the audience: if he is writing for a journal whose audience largely adhere to phenomenology as the theoretical framework of research, he modulates his methods accordingly; on the other hand, if he is writing for a journal that strongly adheres to the positivist tradition, he has no shame to adjust his methods that way, too. So, at least for some researchers, it is a personal choice. I must also add that it is quite irrelevant in some situations as to what your world-view is. For instance, if your research agenda is clearly demarcated as 'project the demand for clean drinking water for the next ten years', irrespective of your worldview, you pretty much tend to adopt the same method.

Q: Can you give any special tips on manuscript preparation for journal submission?

While the old school still thinks that document preparation programs like LaTex are still relevant, most of us tend to type in plain MS office or an equivalent software. If you plan to collaborate with other researchers, it is always better to use online versions of these software. Personally, I use a lot of Google Docs which allows me to 'live collaborate' with my coauthors. If you or your library has subscription, EndNote, RefWorks, etc, can be used for reference management. Also, Web of Science by Thomson Reuters is a good source to identify relevant research papers. Again, personally, I tend to use Zotero for referencing and citation management: it integrates very well with Google Scholar search engine which in turn can, if properly configured, directly access full papers from your library database (I know Mendeley is an equally good alternative). If you plan to submit your paper for the editorial consideration in another journal than the one you originally planned for (say, as a result of the rejection by this journal) and if this second journal follows a different citation convention, changing citations can become too difficult unless you use one of the above referred software. I also use add on spelling-grammar checkers than depending upon the in-built capabilities of programs like MS-Word. My personal suggestion is to use Ginger.

It is also very important to follow each journal's 'guidelines for authors' and, if available, guidelines for reviewers. Please remember to keep a healthy relationship with the coordinating editor of your manuscript-even if the review results are negative.

Q: I am doing my PhD on cybernetics applications in management. My problem is that I cannot continue to work focusing upon my stated research objectives. Already, I have changed my topics, research problems, hypotheses, methods, and ...what not! ... so many times. Does that speak something about me?

A: It does. However, not always negatively (as you might want me to say). Many a time, people might think that you are not a serious research scholar. You might also be criticized for 'lack of depth'. According to me, at least in some cases, research is like chasing a moving target - especially when the field you work on is dynamic and is in a state of flux. You necessarily have to change. In a more ordinary scenario, I have seen a lot of good researchers changing their topics just because they find (mostly during the literature review stage) that the issue they tackle: 1) has already been solved by someone else; 2) is not as important either for theory or for practice as originally imagined; 3) the resource commitments required to carry out the study is more than what was initially thought; 4) a new critical and time-sensitive research issue has been identified and you are forced to keep the less important one in the back-burner. If you have a legitimate reason like one of these, I would say, please go where your heart calls you and do what gives you intellectual joy. But, if you find that you have been shifting gears with nothing tangible to 'show people' over a significant period of time, that might work against building a strong resume - very important in the early stages of career.

A related problem is the forced imposition of disciplinary bounds upon the budding researchers. Many young researchers come up with research proposals that would put them in a situation of 'neither here nor there'. I myself am a very good example here. Custodians of traditions would want to see neat classifications and it is very difficult to classify me either as a business researcher, a social psychologist, a geographer, or an environmentalist. Even when I think of myself as a business researcher, I have problems to identify my specialization: is it marketing, human resources, or just general management? It is sad the academic community forces specialization, even when almost everyone knows that the nature of knowledge is largely holistic.

Nature, Society, Profit (NSP): Intellectual Dishonesty of the Opponents of 'The Triple Bottomline'

This is a topic that keeps getting repeatedly abused by pundits. Today, we had a repetition of the same. Brain breaking discussions - but, almost no one noticed the following arguments I raised by means of a short comment. I thought to rephrase it here:

1. You took a student loan for your education; if you use that as a reason to justify your toiling for the bank for the rest of your life (oh, you won't die if you are like a corporation), I would call you a fool. In the first place, never ever take loans from such banks that want you to toil for them. And, even if you take the loan, never ever listen to the brainwashing attempts by smart guys that say it is immoral and unethical if you don't toil for them. I believe the bank should be paid back the premium with a decent interest (I wish if some of these banks said: well, we don't care about not getting back our principal as long as you could convince us that you, with the support of the money we gave you, made the world a better place to live). Beyond this, it's none of their business to ask you what you do with your talents.

2. In the above narration, I used the example of an individual. However, the logic is equally clear for corporations. While paying rent for the capital is a good (and often expected) gesture, calling that the meaning of existence of a corporation is, well, very demeaning. A business need not (and should not) be a machine that exists to perennially toil for the betterment of shareholders alone. Well, you should give back to your parents for all the goodness that they bestowed upon you: but, your life should not end up serving only what they consider important (Thank God, other than a few Wall Street parents, no one would want their kids to do that). At times, you may also have to challenge them if they are evidently wrong.

3. Sense-making in life is vital not only for individuals but also for corporations. Above all, what a corporation is other than a meeting together of individual minds! I cannot figure out the minds of people who get offended when individuals do not care for nature and society but get offended when corporations DO care for nature and society. Externalities are like you father a monster and then ask the society to deal with it. Forget if shareholder profits increase or decrease as a result of leading a meaningful life, forget the absence or presence of regulatory pressure for the triple bottom line sustainable business practices: what I want to say is that you should do it just because it is the right thing to do, something that makes your life worth living. Corporations, better avoid shareholders who do not care for you, or be prepared to live a mean, worthless, and slavish life!

Potential shareholders, this is your opportunity to invest in companies that serve the environment and communities while also concerned about your investment. Please don't tie the corporations to do things just for your singular selfish interest of monetary profit maximization. The triple bottom line is the best single bottom line. Life is precious, for everyone!

How I Reconciled myself with the Triune God of the Christian Faith

God IS. Yes, that is the true nature of god, a nature that is not amenable to classifications and definitions. The true nature of god does not imply anything but simultaneously does encompass everything. A gleam of the nuances of this can be accessed via statements like:

God said to Moses, "I AM WHO I AM. This is what you are to say to the Israelites: 'I AM has sent me to you.'" - Exodus 3:14.

I am the Alpha and the Omega, the First and the Last, the Beginning and the End. – Revelation 22:13

1. *God the Holy Spirit is the consciousness of god.* Since when god has begun to get that omniscient, omnipresent, consciousness? When did god begin to be self-aware? May be, coincidently with the beginnings of the cosmos. The essential point is The Holy Spirit is not created by god, it just came into being along with the creation of time and space.

The Holy Spirit is impersonal. But, the effects of its presence will appear in the person upon whom it works. The Bible says in Galatians 5:22, "But the fruit of the Spirit is love, joy, peace, patience, kindness, goodness, faithfulness, gentleness, self-control; against such things there is no law". It is the Holy Spirit that transforms sons of man into sons of god!

2. *God the Son is the will of god working through man.* When the Holy Spirit 'works' upon the evolved organisms (a.k.a. humans), they become sons of god, acting out the will of god, with material force, in the material world. Generally, the Bible reflects the view that the Holy Spirit works only with those humans who are prepared. And, they become sons of god. Sons of god are the operational presence of god in the human society, the means through which the 'actions of god' happen as they are in relation to the human kind. The Holy Spirit as an impersonal force has no bias as to where the goodness of god be restricted to. Ideally, the Holy Spirit should work through every man and every man be made sons of god.

Even though the Holy Spirit is impersonal, its fruit, God the Son, is a personal experience. Jesus is a son of god, a son of man that prepared himself utmost for the Holy Spirit to work.

Does god control the freewill of man such that some sons of man prepare themselves to be more appropriate recipients of the blessings of the Holy Spirit? No. The Bible generally is reflective of the view that god takes only a correctional view rather than a controlling view when it comes to the day-to-day dynamics of the various natural phenomena, including the human will. The blueprint of the cosmos may have evolved by itself 'in the course of time'. So, if Jesus has become the most prominent of the sons of god, it may not have been the premeditated wish of god. The Bible talks at various places about sons of god, children of god, etc., making it clear that god does not necessarily have only one son to be called 'The Son'.

3. *God the Father is the voice of god as heard to man.* The Holy Spirit often works silently, without even the sons of god in which it works not conscious about it; yet, at times, the imperative of the Holy Spirit is 'heard' in the man as 'voice from the above'. God the Father is, at any time, the highest sense of material equivalence that a son of god can sensually experience what the true nature of god is. The Holy Spirit is impersonal, God the Son is personal, and God the Father is super-personal.

The fact that God the Father is an embodied perception does not make Him any less real, just as the photograph is of something real is not a mere imagination. It is important to understand that not every son of man may see God the Father in the same embodied form, or not every one of them may see him at the same time and at the same place, although these are possible in accordance with the dynamics with which the Holy Spirit is working in each one.

At the peak of the activity of the Holy Spirit in you, you identify yourself closely with god, within the limitations of your human condition. The best possible way you can identify with god is by means of a felt equivalence with God the Father. The mystery of this unravels in the Bible verses like "I and the Father are one" (John 10:30), "That they all shall be one, just as you, my Father, are in me, and I am in you, so that they also shall be one in us" (John 17:21), and "But those that received him, to them he gave authority to become the sons of God, even to them that believe on his Name" (John 1:12).

In summary, god IS. Also, God the Father, God the Son, God the Holy Spirit, etc., are true representations of god, with their validity restricted to only certain realms. God is triune, but there is nothing that restricts his grace to the trinity.

'The Present is the Only Reality'? Really? Shattering the Assumptions

Assumptions:
1. There are infinite space units (or, simply, objects).
2. The 'present' is a singularly pointed, commonly shared, objective reality for all the space units. Yes, it's a point located in the temporal axis, plane, or n-dimensional temporal space (we don't know and it doesn't matter). For simplicity sake, imagine the present as the mid-point of a circle that constitute the temporal plane.
3. The present has a unique 'temporal quality' that makes it uniquely 'the present' and distinguishes it from the past and the future.

Analysis:
1. In order for all the infinite space units to be in the present, all these units try to grab the unique temporal quality that characterizes the present. Imagine bees trying to fly into be as close to the queen bee as possible.
2. Just as no more than one object can occupy the same space (spacial property) simultaneously, no more than one object can acquire the same time (temporal property) simultaneously.
3. The aforementioned scenario leads to only one object occupying the 'point in time' that makes up the present and all other objects accumulate around that object. Some very close, some pretty close, and some even far-far away.
4. The aforementioned scenario results in the idea of 'relative presents', meaning that the present is different for different objects. The 'present' for any object may be measured in the form of the 'temporal distance' between the point that makes up the present and the location of the object under study.
5. A group of objects located close to one another, irrespective of their temporal distance from the point that makes up the present, might feel that they share the same present. This is because the temporal distances among these objects are short. Objects located farther away from each other will be living in significantly different 'presents'.
6. Now, re-imagine: it was an arbitrary suggestion to give any particular point the privilege of being able to define the present. Just remove that privilege! Now, with no bias, any of the infinite temporal spots out there could equally qualify to define the present. No particular vantage point, other than that objects that find themselves located at proximate temporal points would think they share the same present.

Conclusion:
The preliminary assumptions are contradicted. The present is not a commonly shared singular reality for everyone. Or, the present doesn't exist as a unique something 'at a point in time'.

Can Seers Predict the Future?

IS FORTUNE TELLING POSSIBLE? Let's do a simple thought experiment. Imagine the life cycle of an organism (O1) is only a nanosecond. It takes birth, grows, matures, declines, and dies in a nanosecond. As a human being (O3), on your timeline, you don't even see this as part of your reality. May be, with a high powered nanoscope you could peep in and observe this - but, only with a substantial time delay. Thanks to your limited sensory and processing capacity, you will see the birth of this organism a few seconds after its death. However, imagine also that there is another organism (O2) that lives almost along the timescale of O1. This organism can see the life cycle of O1 with a time delay, say, of only a few microseconds.

So, we now have three time scales: that perceived by O2, that perceived by you (O3), and the actual time scale lived by O1. By the time you know about the death of O1, that is, when it is the 'present' for you, it would have long become 'past' for O2. With the same logic, O2 saw the death of O1 when it was still 'future' for you.

Now, imagine also that O2 can communicate this news to you in a few microseconds. Remember, your own native faculties, even with the advanced gadgets you have, are yet to see the event. But, you hear of it from O2. Then, after a few more seconds, you see the event for yourself on your nanoscope.

Finally, imagine that O2 is not just a random organism. Yes, for our thought experiment, O2 is a specially gifted human being, a true seer!

Wasn't O2 a credible (mis)fortuneteller for you, O3? Does this thought experiment at least suggest the possibility for 'miracle workers' who could fore-bring the future for you?

Further food for thought: if there is no single and generally shared 'present' for everyone, that appears at the same time for everyone, isn't it foolish to declare 'the present is the only reality'? Isn't the idea of present itself an illusion that creates the other two illusions - of the past and of the future?

Emergent Phenomena and 'Leap of Faith'

The array of VIBGYOR colors that transform into white on Newton's color disk is an emergent phenomenon. You could generate white by various means, including by just painting white color onto the disk. You know that you can generate white by rotating the disk, but by seeing the white on the disk you cannot necessarily conclude that the white color emerged by means of the rotation of the disk. The relation from the disc VIBGYOR colored rotation to the white color formation is indeed 100% predictable; yet, from the white color back to the disc rotation is not. In other words, Newton's color disk can generate the emergent color of white, if rotated above a minimum speed; but, not every white colored disk that we see is the result of a transform from the VIBGYOR pattern.

We can only conjecture the actual origins of many emergent phenomena. It is possible that the causal chain of an emergent phenomenon is known only to an observer who actually partakes it. There is a 'leap of faith' between the causes and the effects associated with emergent phenomena.

One good example to understand this issue is that of 'faith' itself. The person who has faith has no difficulty in believing in it because he knows the actual causal chain that transformed him. The faithful have no problem with their faith because they lived through the 'leap of faith' chasm mentioned above. But, for an external observer, faith could be explained by means of multiple equally valid conjectures the least believable of which probably is the 'leap of faith' narrative.

Summary: While we can create an emergent phenomenon with a forward explanation, no emergent phenomenon has a single privileged backward explanation.

Conceptualizing Demergent Phenomenon

A demergent phenomenon is a phenomenon that emerges from the 'vacuum' created by the receding from one another of phenomena currently joined together. Demergence is the semantic opposite of emergence. Certain phenomena, when they come together leaving their natural states, create an emergent phenomenon. Likewise, a phenomenon that in its natural state is the sum of multiple phenomena will create a demergent phenomenon when it disintegrates and its constituent phenomena drift away from each other. If an emergent phenomenon is a positive reality, a demergent phenomenon is a negative reality.

I feel deeply that many phenomena that we experience are detergent in nature, but I cannot readily think of an example. (May be, the intangible presence left by a departed soul? Or, the hole left by an electron? Or, isn't the universe in its current state a demergent phenomenon - demergence from the big bang, when phenomena began to separate from each other, along with the expansion of the universe?). Why not someone else take this train of thought forward! Don't worry, no need to attribute anything to me.

Life and Causality

Life is a natural counter-force to the force of natural causality. Life, wherever it is present, tends to moderate causality. Thus, life gives us the possibility of freedom, the potential to break predefined causal chains and carve our destinies. Would the causal forces have created life, something that would later constrain their omnipotence?

Or, are these two forces the children of a common pre-natural parent force? Or, are these merely the diverse appearances of the same force that founded and still propelling the universe?

More food for thought: Isn't the story of the Tower of Babel in the Bible (or, Prikruti and Purusha in the Hinduism) a representation of the strains between life and causality?

George, Babu P.

The 'Criminal' Nature of Love

Love by nature is a criminal act; it is the need to get into the deepest private spaces of another individual, without first seeking permission. Love is custom-made for that one and only other individual and the lover is an unsettled lunatic until such custom-made love is delivered to its perfect recipient.

In cases where the other individual takes such intrusion as a stimulation rather than as an irritation, the potential crime metamorphizes into a sweet experience for both the parties. That's all!

Yet, alas, the saddest part is that reciprocated love becomes rotten and loses vitality and sheen not too later. It's a fully ripe flower that is just one step away from extinction. Unreturned love, on the other hand, is very painful. Yet, it is full of life and youthful unpredictability. It takes wonderful forms - poems, paintings, and sculptures - so that the rest of the world too might enjoy the complex undercurrents of its depth. Thus, while the right recipient for which love was originally carved loses out, unreturned love leads to the wider good of mankind. And, the poet in me sang:

Since I can't have you,
And since I won't have you,
I stored all that I can, of you,
In the safest vaults of my memory.

The innocence of your thoughts,
And, the simplicity of your smile,
The sweetness of your words,
And your sweat's intense fragrance,
The sincerity of your kindness and care,
That I felt every moment, without exception,
The pace and rhythm of your heartbeats,
Faint sounds of which I heard but rarely,
The waviness of your movements,
And, snaps of you, from every angle possible.

All these and more I stored,
In the safest vaults of my memory,
So that I can have you,
At my leisure and pleasure,
When I can't have you,
And, when I won't have you.

My Miscellaneous Thoughts about the Perils of the US Healthcare System

Certain things about the system cannot be left unsaid.

- The word 'medical' has overpowered its (kind of) antonym 'health', in almost every country in the world and more so in the US. Medical research is no longer considered by most people to be a net positive generator of value and medical professionals (in particular, big pharma companies) are disrespected by the majority. It's a shrewd, opportunistic business to be in this profession.

- Cost is one of the least valued factors considered in the clinical research and practice. Every major player talks of the need for maintaining cutting the edge quality. Interestingly, minimizing cost is not a consideration in the quality equation. It seems like everyone but the patient benefits out of this convenient arrangement. And, the naive American patient is successfully illusioned into thinking that the high price they pay is inevitable for the high quality of service they deserve. If value is a fundamental characteristic of the US healthcare system, do providers demonstrate value when no one listens and protests? I seriously doubt.

- It's the health insurers that play the game and control it. Patient is a pawn. The collusion between big pharma, the insurers, and to some extent hospitals, (and, to a great extent the bureaucratic-political class) determines the fate of millions of Americans who badly need health care support. Desirable health outcomes are 'jointly defined' (doesn't that make you feel good?) by everyone together, but the patient. I must add a caveat that hospitals are not always in the main colluding group. They are often forced to join the bandwagon and react favorably to the interest of the industry.

- Most public health data are outdated; big data analysis contradicts many traditionally held views.

- The healthcare industry spends more time and effort on governance and transaction related tasks (politicking within the system - "you scratch my back, I will yours" - than to make affordable breakthroughs. This is a deteriorated version of the 'industrial marketing' point of view and it needs to be changed for more consumer centric marketing.

- A freely accessible data driven marketplace of ideas and solutions in healthcare is a need of the hour. Knowledge symmetry can cure many illnesses within the system.

- Many US medical schools are 'fame trapped': they live in the laurels history accorded to them without taking enough care to maintain the background conditions that first led to name and fame

- Simple business sense is not prevailed when the system does not allocate resources appropriately: diabetics is one of the major 'cost centers', but resource

81

allocation to deal with it does not match anywhere.

- In the US, healthcare costs are politically negotiated figures among the major forces that rig the system.

- The US healthcare system should have 'open senses' to understand innovations and changes elsewhere. Sometimes, followers might have something their leader should emulate. Say, many developing countries have developed schemes for highly cost effective care and there is nothing wrong in assimilating aspects from such systems.

- Unwanted level of sophistication in the level of patient privacy has increased the cost of treatment, much beyond the benefits of maintaining such degrees of privacy.

- Current technology permits personalized, customized, evidence based, medicine and treatments (eg: implanting biometric sensors in the bloodstream that can continuously feed a 'machine learning system' with vital data) without reducing economies of scale. However, this opportunity is not used much.

- The windows of opportunities provided by telemedicine and medical tourism are not sufficiently capitalized by the hospitals or insurance companies here in the US. With lowering transportation and communication costs, advantages of medical tourism are more and more visible - but, nothing much is done. Among other things, US based hospitals should consider going abroad and start shops there. Let those American medical tourists going to Thailand receive treatment in a Mayo clinic located in Phuket (at a much lower price than back at home!)! Let telemedicine be used such that longhaul travel is used only for the key treatment and not for pre-post consultations. All these said, many hospitals are reluctant to try foreign waters mainly because they know that corrupt foreign governments and their middlemen wield a lot of undesirable control and that it is easier to fail on your core duty in such an environment. The exit cost is exorbitantly high, if something goes wrong.

- If anything, it's the 'generic medicine' that is doing the fine act to help avoid a total collapse of the US medical system. Many brand name pharma companies have creatively used the generic space to extend the life cycles of their branded products. The thought is "why not do it in-house rather than letting Walmart do it".

- One major problem with unbranded generic medicine, however, is that its quality is a function of regulator oversight. Given the commodity nature, generic manufacturers have nothing much to lose from poor quality.

My Graduation Speech, 1998

I was going through some of my early writings stored in a ZIP folder and came across this gem. I wrote the following (unfinished) graduation message in 1998 to be published in my undergraduate college magazine. I can't remember why; for some reason, it never saw the light of the day.

It's quite funny when I read it now. It was written at a time when I had a very intense Christian spiritual orientation to life. Yes, it 'is not' me but it 'was' me. Dream On!

My dear fellow students,

We are the first graduating batch of our newly established college. We are the first batch of the ambassadors BPC College is sending out to the world and hence we are truly privileged. I meditated over the last few days and decided to give the following message as guiding principles for myself and possibly for all my friends graduating this year.

1. Find joy in the process of learning, irrespective the outcome of learning. The most valuable and lasting outcomes of learning might come out of your failures: taking a personally meaningful reflective approach to your failures often yield valuable lessons for life. In that way, failure is rarely the opposite of success but rather a ladder to a bigger success.

2. Develop a personal philosophy of life, inspired by the Holy Book and our Christian traditions. You have ample degrees of freedom to shape your future within the broader set of guidelines given by these. Each of us has a unique calling and good education should not be to make copycats.

3. Being selfish is generally a sin. However, at times, you need to strive selfishly for selfless pursuits. When you associate your personal goals with the divinely inspired goals of humanity, your selfish pursuits transform themselves into selfless pursuits for the humankind. Herein lies the true roots of leadership, too. When you do this, you become the voice of the humankind and in that process automatically become a leader.

4. Your knowledge becomes valuable only when it adds value to the lives of others. Unfortunately, many people use their knowledge as a weapon to the disadvantage of others. This competitive approach has resulted in an innumerable

number of problems, of which the most serious one probably is the segmentation of humanity into narrowly focused groups. In most cases, there is nothing wrong with knowledge in itself; the problem lies in how one interprets and employs it. Beware that when your knowledge destroys your neighbor, you might well be playing the fiddle of the devil.

5. Humbleness should only increase with the acquirement of each extra bit of knowledge. A better learned person understands better how infinitesimally little our knowledge is about the marvel of creation. You should be proud that you have worked hard and became part of an exclusive club, better suited to serve the society and to further God's will. But, your pride should not make you blind; it should not cause you to demand privileges at the suffering of others.

6. Never stop your thirst for knowledge. You will only marvel how infinitely beautiful the mind and how abundantly merciful the heart of your creator is. There is always some vacuum in your knowledge let God fill in those gaps. Prayfully immersing yourself with these thoughts is one of the best ways of meditation.

7. Knowledge is a destabilizing force. The history of knowledge shows that each stage of instability after preceding stages of stability brings in better and more advanced stages of stability. This is true both at the individual and at the societal levels. Yet, the journey through knowledge can temporarily test your faith. Some of the findings of scientific research, if separated from the 'bigger picture' can make you question the foundations of your faith. If that happens to you, just be aware that you are not alone. These are testing times, but don't panic nor do anything out of frustration. Take a deep breath, calm yourself, take a step back, look at the bigger picture once again, and I am sure you would see yourself again standing upon your foundations.

Let me wind up, and may the pathways to the future be full of joy and blessings!

Newton's First Law, for Managers

Yes, the Law of Inertia is something that managers should really give heed to.

If you ever tried to pull a stranded car, you know that the force to be applied to make it begin to move from its state of rest is much higher than the force you would apply once the car begins to move. If it were not for friction, you would also have applied a lot of force to finally stop the moving car.

In layman's terms, Newton's First Law (Law of Inertia) says that objects love to continue to remain in their current state - be it rest or uniform motion. An object continues to do whatever it happens to be doing unless a force is exerted upon it. If it is at rest, it continues in a state of rest. If an object is moving, it continues to move without turning or changing its speed.

Change is not natural and force is required in order to bring in change. This is more easily understood than the consequence of it. You need force even to reverse (an undesirable) change, back to the state of normalcy. However, this aspect is least understood when managers do things 'for a change', without much forethought. Say, you introduce a deep price cut with a view to multiply your market share, the lowered price becomes the norm, then you realize it is not sustainable, and then forced to roll back the price cut with a much 'greater force'. A better example comes from the chitchats I frequently have with some of my 'change manager' friends - Say, you introduce some change in the organizational culture with a great force to overcome the widespread resistance against change, the change management initiative backfired, and then you try to (failingly) bring back the ship to the early state - if your ego permits.

The word 'force' I use here is a proxy for all the expenditures: financial, technological, educational, negotiational, intimidational, etc. Oftentimes, these resources are in limited supply and there are opportunity costs. The generally heard advice that "lets' just do it" often oversimplifies the situation. In many situations, you cannot tinker with the outcomes on an incremental level or easily roll back a change. Change should not be attempted except by those who can see the pathways and consequences ahead.

George, Babu P.

Nodes of Happiness and Sorrow and their Deceptive Power in Life

In 2008, I visited Rishikesh in the lower Himalayas. The following is what I heard from a saintly man I happened to meet while being there:

We are experience seeking organisms. The algorithm that drifts us over the axis of time is full of subroutines in order to ensure that we don't miss any good experiences.

Time is both uni-dimensional and multi-dimensional. In terms of the 'flow of time', we perceive it as uni-dimensional, directed at 'future'. However, within the 'real' time perceived above, we also believe and act as if time has multiple dimensions and directions. Within the unitary dimension and direction of time, we find nodes of experiences dispersed across a multitude of virtual 'sub-temporal' dimensions and directions. When we move to the future carried by the unitary temporal dimension, we try to grab some of these nodes of experiences (nodes of happiness) while trying to stay away from some others (nodes of sorrow). In fact, our sensation of the flow of time comes largely from the acrobatics associated with our attempts to relate positively and negatively with these nodes of experiences.

However, what most people do not learn is that this is sheer deception (maya): Both the nodes of sorrows and the nodes of happiness are mental constructions and the mind constructs them in such a way that embracing one of them will invariably make you embrace the other. Not that mind is an evil force but that, by the very definition, happiness or sorrow cannot be created without creating the other. Any discerning person can see that these twins are attached to the same string and that they move together in complex ways. The connection is not simple or straightforward, but would surely equalize over any infinitely large tossing in magnitude. Hence, anyone sojourning the nodes of happiness should be anticipating nodes of sorrow or did have some of them in the past. Also, unless you escape yourself from this deceptive chains of happiness and sorrow, you would never experience your true self. Your true self need not seek joy - it is full of incredible joy itself.

A true ascetic is someone who distances from these nodes and focuses upon the 'dimension-free instants' with which the neutral axis of the flow of time is constituted. That is why true ascetics do not feel pleasures or pains the way we experience them. The taste of these instants along the neutral axis of time is not indifference but rather divine bliss. In that experience, the consumer and the consumed become one, being and nothing become indistinguishable, and the infinity contracts into the instant.

So, my dear boy, please share this truth with others! And, follow my example, when you begin to feel the call from within!

Loss or Gain?
I never won,
So, why then is this feeling of loss?
Oh, yeah, I aimed to lose,
I played to lose,
Knowing all well, I would,
As if wanting, I must,
So, shouldn't that be victory,
This feeling of loss?

The Philosophy of a Teacher-Researcher: Some Personal Reflections

A Little Background

My career is a way for me to attain personal excellence by means of discovering and disseminating knowledge for the advancement of humanity. As a career academic, I do research, teaching, academic administration, community service, consulting, and various allied extension activities - each of these reflects who I am and what I aspire to be.

As a young boy, I used to wonder "What do I want to be?". The answer, in my personal life, was clear from the very early on. I wanted to consume (and be consumed by) the immense beauty of this life gifted to me by destiny. For me, it meant discovering the hidden principles, structures, and relationships that make things work in peculiar ways. I believe in the platonic ideal of a philosopher as someone who can liberate the 'prisoners' from the world of immediate sensations and lead them to the more fundamental world of ideas. Ideally, every research oriented program should aim at developing philosophers capable of doing the same, within the field of inquiry of each.

The intricate interconnectedness of life made any attempt from my part to 'specialize' difficult. That said, I realized that life was short and resources at hand were limited: consequently, I decided to primarily focus upon understanding a particular aspect of human life: the life of human beings as consumers. So, for the most part, I am now a consumer researcher. However, I believe that truth and meaning lie in the whole and am always keen to relate my studies with other knowledge fields. You might conveniently call my attitude as one of interdisciplinarity, transdisciplinarity, counterdisciplinarity, or postdisciplinarity.

My Teaching

As a teacher, I believe that learning should lead to the enrichment and elevation of the human spirit. This cannot be achieved if we adopt a model of instruction that views learning as the process of picking pieces of knowledge from the external world and planting them to the world internal to the learner. Knowledge should be meaningful: the best way to make it so is by helping the learner to understand the value of his learning in the context provided by a subjectively meaningful teleology.

A few words about my teaching method: I adopt an eclectic composition of instructional strategies. For a typical course of study, you will find me using lectures, case discussions, term papers, micro-projects, and experiential exercises. My experience tells me that this blend ensures the development of some novel understanding in addition to the dissemination of extant knowledge available in standard textbooks. I believe that elementary school students are as capable of knowledge discovery as doctoral students and that nurturing them early in their lives to partake in discovery is vital for a progressive society.

I believe that knowledge, the fundamental building block of the physical, mental, and the spiritual worlds, is revealed to its seeker when the veils of ignorance are progressively removed. My ideal teacher is neither the one who knows everything nor the one who can effectively communicate everything. Instead, an ideal teacher is the one who enlightens the learner, guides him through the path of self-discovery, and achieves enlightenment in that very same process. Personally speaking, I find in teaching yet another way of learning. Quite contrary to the popular perception, this philosophy can be effectively applied to teaching and learning in any discipline and at any level of schooling.

Student Oriented Education

Marketing theory informs us that 'customer is the king' and a straight interpretation of this dictum is that teachers should be subservient to the students. A lot of educational institutions, especially the 'for profit' ones, have embraced this philosophy verbatim and have redefined the role of teachers as servants. However, marketing theory also talks about search, experience, and credence services, based on the difficulty level to measure the impact of a service by the customers. Positing that education is largely a credence service the utility of which cannot be grasped by the students in the near-term future, we can at least moderate the profaneness of the master-slave relationship implied by the 'customer is king' logic.

I believe education as a service embodies elements of all these three categories but also goes beyond them. It is not only the customer who does not know well the immediate impact of learning but also the service provider. The teacher does not have a significantly better vantage point in judging the impact of teaching and learning than the student. This makes education a journey together, charting a course in response to the nuances surrounding the student, the teacher, the educational system, and the macro environment. Such an approach to education focused on co-creating experiences will make learning personally meaningful and will lead to the molding of a generation of original thinkers and not copycats. Thanks to technology, in particular a variety of cutting edge e-learning solutions, mass customization in education now a possibility.

In 'Practical' Terms

In the above backdrop, a good teacher should make his students feel that they are cared for and that their concerns are given extreme importance. A warm working relationship with students, one that does not go beyond the border of acceptable professional conduct, is vital. In the classroom, the teacher should display sufficient command over the subject being taught. Yet, he should be humble enough to behave as a steward to inquiry. Providing meaningful course expectations and then working hard to meet or exceed those are important keys to student satisfaction. It is also imperative that teachers be good communicators and time managers.

Questions and Answers: Miscellaneous Issues on Higher Education

A couple of weeks back, I was invited to virtually participate in a Swiss based think-tank that brainstormed on a wide variety of issues affecting higher education. Interestingly, many of the issues that came up for discussion in this forum resonated in the Lilly Arctic Conference 2013 that I attended this week, too.

As a representative member of the expert panel for the United States, I was asked to address the following:

Q1: A major complaint about the US system of education is that the students are not intrinsically motivated to learn. They are driven primarily (and in most cases, only) by the extrinsic value addition that a program of study would give them. Is that true?

Ans: I do share your concern in this regard. I have not come across any large sample study that supports your statement. However, anecdotes attest to your 'complaint'. Yes, a rich blend of extrinsic and intrinsic motivational bases will be ideal. Trusting intrinsic motives alone is a path of extreme unpredictability: intrinsic motivation is like creativity; it comes and goes in waves. Most students would not complete a course in a timely manner if that is the only motive.

Actually, a better way to describe student motivation is to use Herzberg's two factor theory found in the industrial psychology - organizational behavior literature. Herzberg distinguishes hygiene and motivational factors. In terms of student learning, getting a good grade or a high paying job are hygiene factors whereas intellectual stimulation or personal growth are motivational factors.

The good news is that we can somewhat transform many extrinsic motivational factors into intrinsic ones. I have been an advocate for 'narrative grading': The instructor may report 1-3 sentences long qualitative comments along with the number/letter grades. The same may appear on the transcript, too (if the student chooses to). Say, if it is a course on research methods, one student may get the comment "she was particularly noted for her skills in conducting focus groups".

Q2: What according to you is the best aspect of the US higher education system?

Ans: Institutionalized educational systems by and large do not have much incentives in promoting meta-cognitive learning in students; meta-cognition enables students to break out of cognitive jails, threatening institutions and even entire nations. The American higher education system is largely free from the clutches of tyranny, at least in comparison with the rest of the world. When I imagine about universities, the immediate expression of my imagination is UNIty-in-diVERSITY. The free market and the diversity it affords are some of the major reasons. Then of course, the willingness of people to go up to a great extent to protect the world views of others whom they do not necessarily agree with (freedom of expression).

Q3: You are a professor of business. What according to you is something that afflicts academic social science -business research the most?

Ans: Plato declared that the role of a philosopher is to liberate the 'prisoners' from the world of immediate sensations and lead them to the more fundamental world of ideas. Ideally, every PhD program should aim at developing philosophers capable of doing the same, within the field of inquiry of each. Unfortunately, one of the first questions asked of a PhD holder these days - including the universities that would want to hire them - is "do you have any practical experience"? I do not say academic researchers need not intervene in the world practice. However, short term orientation is killing the true spirit of academic research. We do need strong DBA like programs to carve out practice oriented researchers.

Q4: Why are some of the world's top-tier universities the evangelists of MOOCs? Shouldn't they rather protect their exclusive turfs by keep restricting entry?

Ans: Well, that is a smart move. Remember, if you do not innovate, someone else would do that and make you irrelevant. It is foolishness to resist Megatrends and be washed away. Better it is to surf at the top of the new wave and keep your leadership position, whatever that might mean. I think Mubarak could survive in Egypt if he could sense the Arabian Spring coming and remake himself as the champion of brotherhood-crazy.

Q5: What do you do to create a culture in your online classrooms?

Ans: In fact, e-learning is very counter cultural. If there is any culture there, that is the culture of flexibility, independence, and autonomy. However, if I analyze your question through a more traditional lens of e-learning, I would say that the process of cultural formation is very time consuming. You cannot create any unique culture within a span of 3-4 months you meet your students in an e-classroom!

Q6: You noted while making one of your previous observations that the research on flip classrooms has got many loose ends. Can you elaborate?

Ans: Yes. For one thing, 'flip classroom' have become a buzzword and a cliche. It is promoted to advance the idea that watching a recorded lecture on a topic by the instructor prior to attending the classroom session on that topic is wonderful and amazing. The proponents say that, this way, the classroom session can be used for more fruitful activities. But, really, is this such a new concept? Well, we didn't have recorded lectures but instructors often used to ask students to "read the textbook and come for a discussion in the class".

I fully agree with the spirit of flipping. But, from the perspective of a typical learner, it would make more sense to listen to the pre-recorded lecture after the classroom session. Lectures are boring. Students are more likely to appreciate the theoretical aspects of a topic communicated via lectures if they are presented with the lectures after immersing them with certain classroom or outdoor based 'active learning' components.

In general, this hangout was a wonderful opportunity for educational thinkers from around the world to share their insights and learn from each other. I wish to share some of the interesting observations made by the other participants in a forthcoming blog post. Stay tuned!

How Overly Focusing upon Tomorrow's Solutions for Today's Problems Causes you to Miss both your Today and Tomorrow

This is not string theory. But, it is amazing that the vast majority among us do not care to understand this critically important idea for a meaningful life.

My psychologist friend from Goa Agnelo Vaz coined the phrase 'masturbating over the lost opportunities' to mean the behavior of those who mentally recover and reconstitute their lost opportunities later in their lives. Such reconstitution gives them a fictitious control over their past and a fictitious kind of happiness - just as the control and happiness being felt by a masturbator - according to Dr. Vaz. Most human beings entirely miss the wonderful opportunities of the moment to live in the richness of the moment by worrying only about the problems that moment has in store for them. A minority among them do not merely worry passively but also devote that moment to search for solutions with the hope that their solutions could help them enjoy similar moments in the future. While you may be tempted by the inherent goodness of this smart minority attitude, that does not help much. The reasons are twofold:

1. Most significant 'moments of the today' are one-upon-a-time events. These moments do not present themselves again in the future. Please realize that a moment of truth is generated out of the co-creation of an event in the external world and you. Even if the event might repeat, 'you' will have changed in the future. A crude example: you don't enjoy the pleasure of driving (and partying) as a late-teenager when you are determined not to buy a low end used car but work on your part-time job harder and harder to accumulate money to buy that high end Ferrari. You might be able to make enough money to buy one by the time you turn 27. But alas, you cannot go back to your teenage to enjoy the moments of truth associated with driving a Ferrari as a teenager.

2. When the future unfolds itself, it unfolds as the present. Yes, it unfolds with new moments of truth with their associated new causes of worries. At 27, it might not be your greatest joy to dash upon a Ferrari with your girlfriend but still it is joyful. The sad part is that you often miss even such secondary opportunities, just because you have new worries of the present to tackle down. Needless to say you missing the brand new key moments of truth in your by-now-habituated constant search for new solutions to new problems. So, at 40, you have the solutions for the 25's problems but, for the most part, you can only masturbate to get a feel of how the lost pleasure would have been if you were to enjoy it at 25! A life of worries create masturbators out of kindred spirits.

What I say is not to sustain an attitude of carelessness. It is vitally important that we solve the problems of the present. Or, they may become far bigger problems in the future. Some such problems might negatively impact not only you but also the entire humanity. I can appreciate the hard work and dedication of a scientist to find a solution to tackle AIDS or global warming - spending a whole lot of time in the labs, entirely at the cost of the other joys of the present. I said 'the other joys' because I know that many scientists do enjoy their work and experience moments of truth in their journey of research. My counsel is aimed at those who cannot spare even fractions of their time to immerse in the present and finally die without 'knowing their being' in the flesh.

Put it another way, my argument is not to seek happiness in the solutions of problems: there is no human solution that does not raise new problems. You miss out the present by searching for the solutions of the present's problems; even if you might get in the future the solutions you sought, that is invariably when the future becomes the new present; and, invariably, these solutions bring forth new problems for you to continue to worry in the new present. What a mess thou hast made of thine life, O mortal man!

This life is a unique opportunity presented to us. We are made of samples of elements spread across this vast universe and probably beyond. It required the confluence of an array of intensely complex processes to create each one of us the way we are. We are the 'distributed brains of the cosmos' with the associated sensory accessories for it to self-aware what it is. If we fail to experience the moments of truth in our lives, we lose out as the creations of cosmos tasked with the aforesaid marvelous objective. The only legitimate and inherently meaningful masturbation is when the cosmos enjoys itself though our moments of truths. Remember, once you dissipate back to the cosmos, you will also get to enjoy the fruits of the moments of truth created not only by you but also by every life forms in the cosmos. Yes, each one of us in this life should devote to make the music of the cosmos merrier by our lives - yes, merrier than when we could enjoy it before we took life in this form.

Now, I believe I should stop worrying about what next to blog and start living in the present. Good bye everyone, for now!

George, Babu P.

When global localization and local globalization meets

In sum, what I am going to propose below is that the recent-most trend of a reversal of more traditional forms of globalization is not anti-globalization but is a facet of the evolving nature of globalization itself, a facet marked by the dialectical engagement between seamless information symmetry and global access to custom-manufacturing technologies. In this new stage of globalization, the world will be fully interconnected (and truly 'global') by the unifying fabric of information flows but will also ring the death knell for globalization as we see it today.

The spirit of Malthus in me tempts me to believe that globalization has limits and the limits are reached when its advantaged are fully negated by it disadvantages. I believe we have already crossed that stage, especially when it comes to the globalization of manufacturing. But again, even the neo-Malthus is short-sighted.

As a case in point, additive manufacturing (3D printing) makes it possible to locally produce anything. The breaking science news yesterday announced that we were able to create 75% of an 'actual' human skull using this disruptive technology. In the not so distant future, we might be able to print a wide range of sophisticated objects 'at home'. I do not find a reason why something that can be computer modelled cannot be 3D printed. Over time, the cost of additive custom-manufacturing systems would also come down and this technology is almost certain to make globalization as 'outsourced manufacturing' obsolete. So, the end of globalization? In other words, will these technologies be the flag bearers of a new wave of localization?

Emphatically, no. The internet has created a globally connected brain of talents. The most valuable wisdom about anything is no longer sought inside a single human brain but rather in this huge network, which shares almost every characteristic of a well-developed organic human brain but a whole lot bigger in terms of information gathering, storage, processing, outputting, and implementation capabilities. This super brain is increasingly getting decoupled from parochial influences and has given the human world a 'common global base' for meaningful local action. Any keen observer would agree, even today, every local action has a global flavor to it.

So, the extreme alternate scenario is this: As the 'thickness' of the aforesaid common global base increases, the global flavor in local actions will only increase and (except in the case of a very limited set of ultra-localized events) might ultimately eliminate the local element altogether. Personally, I believe that the future will be closer to this scenario than the one portrayed in the previous paragraph. Or, better, let's leave that prediction to the crowd-brain in the cloud!

Network Diseconomies of Scale in the Live Online Classroom

As we are taught, a network effect is the effect that one user of a good or service has on the value of that product to other people. When network effect is present, the value of a product or service is dependent on the number of others using it. Metcalfe's law states that the value of a telecommunications network is proportional to the square of the number of connected users of the system. But, does the network effect always happen in the live classrooms? From my experience, it does happen up to a level, then stops and reverses. Yes, yet another bell curve!

Currently, I am teaching an MBA level online class which has got an enrollment of around 30 students. I use Adobe Connect for live interactions. Adobe Connect is a heavy duty video conferencing solution - much more advanced than Google+ hangouts, Skype in the Classroom or other competitors like Blackboard Collaborate and Webex. It can accommodate a limitless number of video-chat participants at the same time. But, I have noticed that the quality of interaction goes down when we have anywhere more than 7-9 participants. In technical terms, this is a 'congestion' issue: a congestion in path that limits the flow of ideas. In actual practice, it is not merely a congestion in the path (traffic congestion), but is also about the limitations of the information recipients.

Recently, I started a research project with the hypothesis that schools with larger student enrollment are more likely to be benefited by means of social media, the key argument being that each student would get a chance to learn from a larger pool. Especially in the synchronous mode of interactions, this hypothesis might not hold true. This is because the technology available to us does not help us much in managing the information overload and the limitations of the human expert (the instructor) in doing an effective job here gets more pronounced as the information overload increases.

Also, with this experience, I am somewhat skeptical of the power of network media, including social media, to expand the quality of education delivery in the live-virtual classroom settings (in the manner practiced currently). If MOOCs are largely successful, that might be due to the fact that they are offered in the asynchronous mode. By that same logic, if large open 'live' classrooms are to be successful, the live video-conferencing interactions should be limited to smaller groups within the larger classroom.

The methodology I suggest for this to happen is that local groups be formed within the larger MOOC framework, with 15-20 students and a local instructor-facilitator for each such group. This refined model will benefit the second and third tier educational institutions around the world whose role would be to create and nurture local nodes and sub-networks within the super-network of MOOC courses. The instructors in these second and third tier schools might want to customize the MOOC course contents and act as accessible local supervisors for the students enrolled in the courses. Implemented this way, it will provide a continued rationale for the existence of 'the small, local, and unique' schools but at the same time helps positively revolutionize the higher education landscape around the world.

The Myth of 'Mass Tourism'. Or, what NGOs and Academic Researchers Misled us into Believing.

So, this is what we have been hearing all along: tourism is evil and mass tourism is the king of it all. The other day, when I advanced at a conference the argument that (at times) many small businesses together create more damage to the ecosystem than a single large business, almost everyone in the audience stared at me as if I were the Attorney General of the Devil. Despite many such bad experiences, I am determined to expose more such fallacies of the default thinking.

Over the last decade, I have gotten quite a large number of wonderful opportunities to interact with tourism dependent resident communities living in (and out of) destination areas around the world. I HAVE NOT HEARD ANY OF THOSE COMMUNITY MEMBERS LAMENTING THAT MASS TOURISM IS EVIL. Well, a little bit of exaggeration here, but no joke and I am very serious. Actually, all the complaints I heard were about those glorified and self-styled independent travelers.

But, why am I right and why the dominant thinking is wrong? Well, I definitely can't explain all the nuances here but the core argument is that PACKAGED-GROUP-MASS TOURISM is the best way to limit tourist flows to certain circuits which also would most likely have developed tourist-centric infrastructure. While mass tourism offers the economic means of survival for tourism destination communities, it also restricts tourist movement beyond the beaten path - reserving the sacred and the authentic to the locals. As one of the Alaskan native students whom I met recently put it succinctly: "We don't have many recreational opportunities for our community members in our nine month long winter; during our short summer, we do want to make some money but not at the cost of backpackers intruding into our backyards and polluting our pristine terrains. Mass tourist rarely go beyond the mainstream routes, they have only limited opportunities to violate the established norms, and they are our best bet."

May be, material for a counter-current research project. Or, maybe not.

Meditations during the Holy Mass on a Beautiful Sunday Morning

Today morning, whilst attending the weekly holy mass, a train of unholy thoughts passed through my mind. Quite unusually, most of the time was occupied with thoughts on evolution.

Isn't the popular statement expressing the 'survival of the fittest' ("the fittest among thou shall survive") a statement of purpose? Scientific statements should not be expressed in such language. While evolution is empirically verified, explanation of 'why it works that way' is, unfortunately, coded in a teleological language.

Also, this language fails the 'test of a good hypothesis': good hypotheses should be falsifiable. There is no way the hypothesis of the survival of the fittest can be rejected. In the event that an 'unfit' species survives, it gets called the fit species (Needless to add the ambiguity associated with terms like survive, fit, etc).

Or, is this only a matter of word-play? Can't we also restate the description of a 'fair coin' in a manner that propose a purpose in nature? As a tutor for high school students long back, I remember explaining to them the fair coin as an expression of nature's unbiased attitude: the purpose of nature is to play the role of an unbiased judge.

Then my mind wandered over a different landscape. While the priest explained the 'Wedding at Cana', he highlighted how miracles work. Immediately, my mind began to dwell upon the consequences of 'localized violations of universal principles' (popularly called miracles).

After a few minutes of fuzzy thoughts, it was concluded that miracles were not possible since 'universal principles cannot be violated only locally'. If a universal principle is to be violated, it should be universally. Remember, I didn't say the process of making wines couldn't be accelerated with appropriate enzymes.

I guess I should stop at this. I don't want to take away all the joys of this lovely day with dull and dreary thoughts.

Now behold, the priest began to serve the final blessings. Have a blessed Sunday!

Is 'Long Term Orientation' Really Long Term Oriented?

Wikipedia talks about it as follows:

"Long term orientation (LTO), vs. short term orientation: First called "Confucian dynamism", it describes societies' time horizon. Long term oriented societies attach more importance to the future. They foster pragmatic values oriented towards rewards, including persistence, saving and capacity for adaptation..."

Wow! Aren't these values to be really proud of; aren't these the things every society should be aspiring for? I would answer with an emphatic NO. My research on 'responsible behavior' in the Eastern and the Western cultural landscapes led me to ask questions such as this: Why are some of the highly long term oriented Asian cultures also some of the least environmentally responsible cultures? (More concretely, why are the Indians and the Chinese much less concerned about issues like global warming, pollution control, and the preservation of biodiversity?). Evidently, short term oriented Western European cultures are significantly more concerned about inter-generational equity than any of the long term oriented Asian cultures.

But, why is this anomaly? Is the basic theory wrong? Ethnography coupled with self-reflection yielded me the following answer: Due to the very nature of long term orientation, long term oriented cultures tend to become insensitive and ambivalent to the impacts their actions might bring about. The concerns and sensitivities of individuals in the long term oriented societies are diffused across a wider time span and as a result these 'lose steam'. This is the result of an interpretative process that takes the argument from "this action has a long range impact" to "the impact at any short duration is minimal".

The above line of thought pretty much explains the rarity of environmental activism in the long term oriented cultures as well. In other words, the concern for long term is suicidal - it makes you fail in the short term and subsequently in the longer term.

Who said you can foster the forest without fostering the trees!

Boltzmann's Constant in Management Theory

Those of you who learned some high school physics would most likely have heard the name of the great physicist-philosopher Ludwig Boltzmann. If not, please read the Wikipedia entry.

While he did many other wonderful things before he hanged himself during an attack of depression at the age 62, he is most remembered for his contributions to the field of 'statistical mechanics'. In layman's terms, what he postulated was that similar macro-level characteristics of two systems do not imply the same micro-level characteristics of those systems. Micro level characteristics of a system might be anything - these could 'average out' and end up creating the same macro-level characteristic shared by another (unconnected) system. By the way, don't you know that two people looking alike aren't necessarily the same person?

His famous formula for entropy is

$$S = k \ln W$$

S=Entropy
k=Boltzmann's constant
W=the number of possible microstates corresponding to the macroscopic state of a system

The above formula informs us that the entropy (the degree of disorder in a system) does not increase linearly or exponentially with the diversity of micro-conditions but only in a logarithmic way (a lot more moderated!).

Two business organizations might share similar macro level characteristics but the micro level characteristics might be drastically different in each of them. Management gurus and consultants just do not get this. They prescribe solutions just looking at the corporate level picture. Their solutions would go like this: "Nike and Adidas share the same macro level characteristics, problem P in Nike was successfully solved by solution S, hence problem P in Adidas should also be solvable with the same solution S." Nothing can be distant from truth than this!

Another application of Boltzmann's study in the management field is that it can help us understand the way organizational cultures develop (I'm sure this is extendable to national cultures as well). Let us imagine if a person has started a business. He founds the vision and mission and lays the foundations of an organizational culture for the organization-in-the-making. Over a period of time, the organization grows with more members but the macro-level organizational culture is very likely to remain pretty much the same despite the fact that the individual organizational members came from diverse walks of life. In order to preserve the macro-level characteristics, what is required of each member is to negotiate and sacrifice some of their micro-level diversity. If the change in entropy S in Boltzmann's equation is akin to the change in the organizational culture, it is true that the possible diversity in the individual level cultures do not heavily determine that change. Nature applies a logarithmic moderation upon that - whether in the physical systems or in the social systems!

The principle of Brownian motion speaks of something similar in the molecular world, according to which the movement of a big particle (e.g. Pollen) in a medium of smaller particles (e.g. water) is due to the instantaneous imbalance in the combined forces exerted by collisions of the big particle with the much smaller liquid molecules surrounding it. In many cases, the combined forces cancel out each other and the big particle remains where it is. However, as time goes, the probability of the big particle to drift from its original position increases. Also, for most observers, what they see is only the movement of the big particle (unless they have better microscopes-and unless they are excessively curious!).

The intuitive metaphor for business organizations from this is pretty clear: the more visible and seemingly manageable drifts that a big organization makes is the resultant of tons of micro level forces that act in mostly unpredictable ways.

An Addition to the Golden Numbers in the Human Body

Like many of you, I too am fascinated by the golden ratio. A lot of measurements upon the human body to find golden ratios focus upon the ratio of distances between body parts. I would like to add one cent to that already extensive literature.

My measurements focus on the ratio of the distance between the nipples and the distance between either one of the nipples and the navel. The ratio of the latter with respect to the former (approximately) constitutes the golden ratio. See for yourself, if you are not convinced.

The isosceles triangle formed by these lines is a golden triangle. In the diagram given below, $a/b=\varphi=1.6180339 \ldots$, or, the golden ratio.

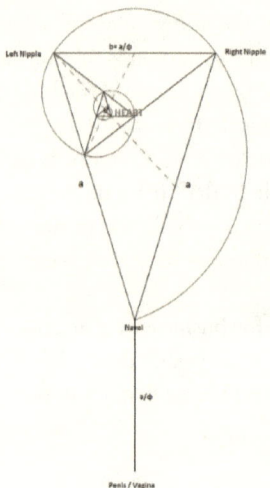

My calculation is based on self-reported measurements gathered from a few male friends. However, I do not find any reason why the same relationship should not hold for the female gender (except that you may have to make more strenuous guesses about the nipple centers).

Interesting, especially in the female case? The belly button is the main connection between a mother and the baby born in her womb; nipples continue to serve that purpose until the child graduates from infancy.

Now, one more golden ratio: the distance between the navel and the penis / vagina upon the distance between either one of the nipples and the navel also turns out to be (close to) a golden ratio.

Also, the diagram above shows a logarithmic spiral touching up on the three corners of the golden triangle. While I do not have the empirical measurements, my intuition compels me to think that the point of origin of this spiral superimposes the 'kernel of the human heart'. I am not an anatomist and I cannot hope to become one in this life - for me, this is a beautiful assumption and if true, would make the human body even more geometrically perfect. Isn't this an aesthetic equation connecting the vital organs of life?

That much craziness for now!

Connection between Religious Beliefs and Managerial Decision Styles

If religious beliefs are based on gut feelings, could managers who are religious depend upon similar gut feelings for managerial decision making, too? Are non-religious managers more likely to adopt information based decision strategies?

Previous research in experimental psychology suggests that religious belief is influenced by one's general tendency to rely on intuition rather than information. A corollary emerging from this based on balance theory is that managers who are religious might make more intuition based decisions than their counterparts who are not religious. The latter group might tend to make more information based decisions.

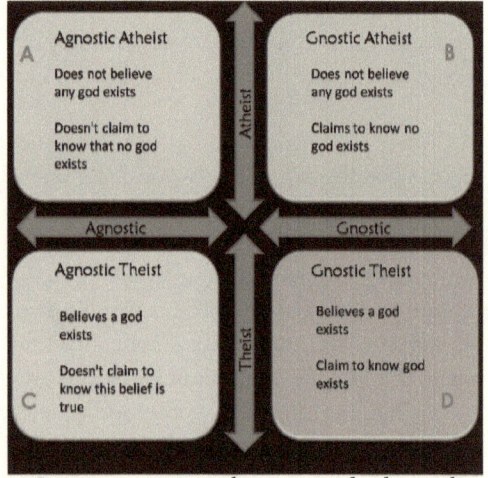

Employing critical incident technique, I am trying to test this potential relationship among business executives.

Preliminary analysis indicates that, while religiosity per se is not a significant predictor of managerial decision style, agnosticism indeed is. Agnostic managers are more likely to depend upon intuition, irrespective of whether they are theists or atheists.

Kindly note that I do not take a position here about the superiority of one of the strategies.

Can you See the Tree and the Forest at the Same Time? The Leadership Challenge

Let me invite you to one of my not-so-scientific classroom experiments recently. The study was conducted among the students of my undergraduate leadership class in the University of Southern Mississippi during 2009.

In layman's terms, the methodology was as follows:

I conceived a major task for the class to achieve and decomposed the task into its various sub-tasks. Without letting them know of the major task, I announced the sub-tasks in a random order and asked the students to achieve them individually. This exercise was completed by the middle of the semester at which stage each of the solutions were subjected to peer-rating by the class. These ratings were used to select the best solution for each sub-task. Later, the students were asked to work on the selected sub-tasks together as a group to achieve the major task. It took them almost two months to put together the pieces and complete the major task to my satisfaction (I must add, it was a wonderful learning experience for me monitoring the complex dynamics of interpersonal and group processes in between!).

After the class made the presentation about the completed project, I gave each student a questionnaire - composed of item statements that would measure how followers rate the leadership capabilities of a leader. Each student rated every other student who participated in the major task fulfillment. Later, I have analyzed the responses. The interesting finding? Why would you have wasted your valuable time reading this if not for that little stuff, right?

Yes, none of the top five leadership score holders figured in the list of students who offered the best solutions for any of the sub-tasks. Generally, students who offered the best solutions for at least some of the sub-tasks were all figured in the middle range of the leadership score - including one 'exceptionally good' student who came as the topper for three sub-tasks. More shockingly, one 'exceptionally bad' student who got the poorest score for two sub-tasks found his position in the list of the top five leaders.

So, what do we make out of this? I guess it is in the title of this post itself (well, you already knew 'the whole is not the sum of its parts'!).

Collectivism = Communally Charged Individualism (Or, What Hofstede Missed)

This reflection stems from my experiences, mainly in India and China.

In international marketing, collectivism is an important factor. According marketing theorists, collectivism means that people in collective societies help each other, people are not as selfish, …, the glorified list is actually very long.

In one of the ongoing (euphemism for 'incomplete forever') studies, I examine the 'willingness to help others in emergency situations' as a special case of the way collectivism is manifested. In the so-called collective societies like India and China, believe it or not, the tendency to care for others in situations that need emergency care is much less than in most 'individualistic' Western European and North American countries. Literature churned out by mass media (Hey, haven't you heard of the recent Chinese hit and run incidents?) and my own personal experiences makes me reaffirm this hypothesis. An American is more likely to help an accident victim crying for help in the roadside than an Indian or Chinese, without looking at that person's color, creed, or group affiliation.

But, collectivism does work. When? And Indian or Chinese will help the victim more than an American, but only if the victim's demographic identity falls under a narrowly defined in-circle (like your family member, village resident, college mate, someone belonging to the same caste or tribe). Asians apply a complicated in-circle Vs out-circle filtering algorithm before deciding to help / forming group affinity.

I have already collected qualitative data based on a number of interviews with Chinese and Indian nationals and these interviews seem to prove my a priory observations. I couldn't complete the project in its entirety since I had to leave China abruptly. Looking forward to the next opportunity.

My Experiments with the Focus Group Methodology

I thought to share with you something I found interesting - from my experience of conducting focus group interviews. Let's compare focus groups conducted using two formats:

1. A single focus group interview conducted with 8 members on a topic of interest
2. A two stage focus interview: in the first stage, you randomly divide the 8 members into two groups of 4 members and conduct focus group interviews with each of these groups independently on the same topic; in the second stage, you conduct the same interview with all the 8 members.

This might seem like a silly alternation. Yet, the results are amazingly superior ... any guess, in which?

Yes, you got it right. The second format is found to be far superior on the following:

1. Significantly less 'groupthink' and pressure to conform in the first stage due to less number of participants in stage 1. Of course, it's a pain to conduct three interviews within time-resource limitations and the availability of participants. But, amazingly so many more ideas!

2. More openness and willingness to arrive at consensus solution ('universal theory'?) in the second stage via discursive process. Participants are willing to assimilate alternate views and modifications upon their original ideas since they are aware that their original ideas were vetted out by only 3 other participants in the first stage. I have noticed the way groupthink works out for good here.

Can we further polish this improvised methodology suggested by me? May be, that's possible. For the record, I did experiment with something I considered even more superior. After the first stage, instead of inviting all the first stage participants to the second stage, I randomly chose 2 out of 4 members of each of the first groups. I must add, the first stage members were made aware that the selection to participate in the second stage was random. Quite interestingly, this process made each of the selected first stage members to feel humbler, less egotistical, and share views that they thought might be interesting - even when such views originated from the participants not selected to participate in the second stage. If you are a qualitative researcher, why not think along these possibilities. You might be able to tinker my solution to make it even better! And, don't forget to share the same with the rest of us.

Predictability, Rather than Probability: Musings of an Amateur Poetical Philosopher

I am not a statistician or a mathematician; rather, I am someone with a deep amateurish curiosity of mathematics and, to a lesser degree, statistics.

Last night, I felt bored and my mind began to wander over the following: When you throw a dice, at what point does the outcome gets decided? This led me to my limited conceptual knowledge of randomness, entropy, and information theory.

I am made to think that, at the beginning of the process of throwing dice, the outcome is fully decided - we can look and verify for sure what the 'face' IS then. However, from that time, this predictability reduces in degrees until it reaches a point of zero predictability when the outcome gets fully un-decided. This is also the point at which all the information about 'what that the face of the dice was immediately before you threw it' is lost. In addition to the dice being fair, reaching this level is an essential condition for the dice-throw to produce a perfectly random outcome.

From the aforesaid peak of uncertainty with infinite entropy and zero information, the dice begins to retreat and degrees of predictability about the final outcome of the dice-throw will begin to emerge and increase. This is a movement from infinite entropy to zero entropy and from zero information to infinite information.

In order to model this, I highlight 13 distinct stages in the process of throwing a dice and associated predictabilities (this is a quasi model with merely indicative values; also, there is no intent to say that there are 13 discreet stages in a dice throw or that the movement from one stage to another is discontinuous).

Stage	1	2	3	4	5	6	7	8	9	10	11	12	1 3
Predictability	1	5/6	4/6	3/6	2/6	1/6	0	1/6	2/6	3/6	4/6	5/6	1

This table might seem deceptively simple and the simplicity might make you neglect the profound principle contained in it. The most profound finding according to me is that the outcome of this random experiment, ceteris paribus, begins to get partially determined in the process that happens between stages 7 and 8. In other words, at stage 8, we can know the outcome of this random experiment with a predictability of 1/6.

You may laugh now, since everyone knows forever that the probability for a particular face to come in a dice-throw is always 1/6. But wait, here we are talking about predictability, the degree of clarity we have about the actual outcome, rather than the probability for any single face to appear. The predictability from an actual observation of a dice-throw is to be distinguished from the probability for a particular face to appear in the experiment. What I say is that this clarity appears in stage 8 and then progressively increases to a certainty of 1 in stage 13 when the dice comes back to rest. In other words, if you are an observer equipped with proper instruments, you can begin to know the outcome of our random experiment in stage 8.

Imperfectly done dice-throws do not reach stage 7. This means, at no stage in the throws these dice go through full randomness. In this scenario, the initial face of the dice immediately before the throw keeps influencing the process throughout and is at least a partial determinant of the final outcome. Based on the predictability value at stage 2 alone, you should be able to partially predict the outcome of this throw.

Another application of this way of thinking is when it comes to random processes that take, say, a million years. By knowing the present predictability value, we should be able to make guesses about the initial state of that random process a million year back. May be, this one is way too farfetched!

Do you want me to mathematically model this process? No, these are the musings of a Poetical Philosopher. And, for me, THE END of what I do is now and here.

A Call for the Return of the Polymath Professor in the Academia

According to the Oxford Dictionary, a polymath is "a person of wide knowledge or learning". He or she has expertise spanning across a wide spectrum of subject areas and domains. It is expected that such expertise should help the polymath to solve complex problems needing the application of transdisciplinary knowledge. Being a polymath, the notion that people should embrace all ideas, is the core around which the idea of a 'renaissance man' was constructed.

However, fast forward, the world has turned upside down. Now, we are at the other extreme: the contemporary world, especially the academia, stresses hyper-specialization. At times, in our hyper-departmentalized academic settings, it is not only that one is hyper-specialized but also that one should desist from the temptation to be interested in any other unrelated areas of inquiry. I know colleagues who were denied prospects not because they were not great in their primary disciplinary domains but because they also had done research in other areas. It is more or less like – *"Oh, you are a professor of Particle Physics; but, I also see you have published a few papers on Mechatronics and even one on Existential Philosophy. Where is your commitment?"*. To aspire to become a 'whole man' will bring myriad troubles for someone in the academia. While sexual promiscuity has almost always been considered unwelcome by the generalized social mass, even merely flirting with different disciplines has become an anathema in the contemporary academia.

Given the vastness of knowledge the humankind has achieved since the times of renaissance, becoming a true polymath has become almost impossible. Most of us just don't have the time, resources, or brain power to become experts in more than a couple of fields. This means, the only way to approximate becoming a polymath is to become a generalist and be ridiculed as a 'jack of all trades'. Finding a place and voice for such people in our hyper-departmentalized universities is hard, if not impossible. Small universities that expect faculty to teach a diverse set of courses in closely aligned disciplinary areas are the best bet for them. So, should you sacrifice all the accolades that your professional growth can fetch for you and become a generalist? I seriously think yes. Especially if knowing, being, and becoming and whole man is an intense call in your life.

It is not only about money and fame; it is about life. Not just to read widely but also to be able to do own research and discover principles in a wide range of areas is a matter of great joy. Seeing firsthand the sublime interconnectedness among apparently unrelated knowledge realms is an artistic experience par excellence. Some of us are restlessly irked for constant doses of this experience throughout our lives. An economist might have to sacrifice some of his professional ambitions by taking some time to do research in another area he is passionate about – say, linguistics or computer programming. But, if it brings him a better sense of life, a greater personal meaning, what else is more important!

Finally, specialization beyond a limit is very hard on some of us: we have minds that just don't agree to immerse deeply into a single micro-specialization. As a business researcher, I just cannot separate marketing, human resource, and finance and constantly focus on only one of these during my entire lifetime – just because that is what my employer expects. At times, I am also tempted to research issues related to philosophy, economics, psychology, sociology, and cultural studies. I am better at seeing the breadth than the depth. These diversions for sure bring frowns from the authority for reasons like *"you are paid to do research on buyer remorse!"*. I actually had to leave one of my previous jobs, partially for this reason. Nonetheless, I am just not capable of a fathomless deep jumping – even if I try.

A well lived life should be characterized by dynamism rather than unidimensional depth. Your relentless quest to expand consciousness across the vast breadth of knowledge need not be subjugated to professional ambitions. If you feel constrained and especially if money and fame are no more important than the aforesaid quest, you should consider a new home for yourself – a place of employment that appreciates and rewards the polymath in you. Look for a university that is serious about providing whole and holistic education to its students. Or, if you are in an Ivy league place and lucky enough, you should initiate to start a center of research for yourself that would tap into integrativist projects requiring application of widespread knowledge and skills.

Variability in Constants and Constancy in Variables: Difficulties in Understanding Social Reality

Everything that we call variable has some basic property which is constant: every variable has (or, is supposed to have) a generally agreed, stable, invariable, meaning. While the *attributes* of variables change, their *essence*, their basic properties, remain constant. Looking this way, what is termed a 'constant' is the particular instance of a variable whose attributes generally take on only one value. In a sense, gravitational constant and acceleration are essentially the same: the difference is that, while acceleration as a general concept can take on any value, gravitational constant can have only one value (9.8m/s).

In physical sciences, velocity and acceleration are variables and also we inter-subjectively agree what these terms mean. However, in social sciences, this is not the case. The inter-subjective agreement is assumed, but it is vastly unrealistic. In our quest to model social sciences after hard physical sciences and make grand theories, we just play down the underlying complexity with the assumption of an inter-subjectively agreed upon reality. Say, in marketing, we claim that the basic essence of customer satisfaction is assumed to be a constant (everyone is supposed to know satisfaction is 'S' and not 'P', 'Q', or 'R'). Yet, it is undeniable that there is some variability even in our understanding of the basic essence of a variable: the idea of satisfaction is not understood and experienced by everyone alike.

So, even when ten people say the are satisfied '4' on a 5 point scale, the subjective experience of satisfaction is not the same for all these ten people. There is significant variability in essence, in addition to the variability in the attribute. Despite this, in social research, lamentably, we singularly focus on variability in the attribute neglecting the variability in the essence. If ten respondents to a survey understand a term like satisfaction in ten different ways, making a conclusion "all the respondents are highly satisfied" would be a vastly misleading judgement.

Calculating the total variability as a product of the essence variability and the attribute variability can increase the value of our understanding of social reality. So, in the case of customer satisfaction, the product of how much customers are satisfied multiplied by how diverse their understanding of what the concept of satisfaction is, gives us that new perspective.

During the scale development process, we perform reliability analysis to weed out items that people don't inter-subjectively agree. In practice, that process takes the soul out of real human experiences associated with the constructs we aim to measure and what remains are mere skeletons without flesh and blood. Ironically, validity in technical terms is established only when all variability in the essence of a construct is weeded out. How valid is that!

In this backdrop, I call for a methodology not to eliminate inter-subjective differences in the scale development process but rather to incorporate them in our judgements during the interpretation phase of the findings of a study.

Emotion Overload, the Neglected Cousin of Information Overload

There exists a lot of literature on information overload. Variously called as infobesity, data smog, infoxication, and information glut, it refers to the difficulty to grasp something because of the presence of too much information surrounding it. The basic idea is that too much information could strain our cognitive resources, causing us to make poor choices. Alvin Toffler in the 1970's popularized it in his well acclaimed book, the Future Shock.

However, apart from a few scant references online, not much mention is found for the term *emotion overload*. Also, the existing references to this term do not have much in common. I believe emotion overload is equally an important concept as its cousin brother information overload. More scholarly attention needs to befall on this: there is an unmet need for it to be developed into a valid construct in the communication literature. Preliminarily, I would like to define it as our difficulty in understanding people and their ideas, caused by the complexity of emotions built around them. This lead to misunderstandings, poor decision quality, and failed relationships.

In particular, emotional overflow has become a huge issue in communication over the social media. We routinely tend to overuse smileys and emoticons in social media communication: this has an entertainment value but could also seriously perplex the receiver of the message. How often do you get an instant message from someone, spiced up with a curious mix of four or five smileys! Smileys are free and we just don't know we are reducing the signal to noise ratio by overloading the message with them.

Even in face to face communication contexts, there is a need to reduce emotion overload. Emotions flavor communications and to some extent add value to it. Some ideas cannot just be communicated effectively without using emotional expressions. In certain cases, our emotions are our message. Sometimes, our emotions are so strong that we cannot stop crying or laughing out loud. Those are quite natural ways to be human. But, concocting emotions to bring in artificial pitch is at its best a kind of entertainment and at its worst sheer deception. So, be mindful enough to communicate your genuinely felt emotions, don't confuse the audience with them.

The world has changed a lot since Toffler's times and right now we are in what may be called the attention economy: attention is the global social currency and communication is a critical means of gaining attention. People competitively overusing informational and emotional expressions in communication should be seen in this context. The irony is that, when everyone does this narcissistically, everyone ends up getting less attention than they would have got before - just because the time available to us or our faculties of brain don't scale up along with the flood of information and emotions.

Small Wins Strategy may be Big Loss Strategy: 'Penny Wise, Pound Foolish' in Management Theory

Management gurus are theory borrowers at their best. In this instance, they borrowed University of Michigan psychologist Karl Weick's ideas on how to tackle social problems, quite unreflectively, and repackaged them as Small Wins Strategy. Professor Weick proposed that most larger social problems could be decomposed into smaller ones that are more realistically solvable. Solving these smaller problems one after the other will help us overcoming larger and seemingly insurmountable social evils.

From there, a Harvard Business Review article published in May 2011 made that grand proclamation: "The power of small wins applies just as well to problems in business.". This journalistic piece refers to a couple of best seller books, but it is not evident if the claim is supported by peer reviewed research. HBR followed this up with a series of related articles. Later, this wisdom seeped into a large number of management textbooks as well. Now, most MBA programs around the world teach this as unchallenged wisdom.

Today, I was reading a comment on Reddit by u/LOOK_AT_MY_POT. It went like this:

"I pay $0.47/roll for the triple ply quilted stuff. My friend who buys one roll at a time from the convenience store pays almost triple that for gas station quality stuff. Say you go through 2 rolls/week. That's an extra $100 I have at the end of the year. Just on toilet paper. Add in paper towels, soap, and other stuff like that, and this man spends $1000 more than I do every year on necessities. He makes 11% of what I do."

What is the problem here? Is the poor person at fault for not being able to afford the big toilet paper packet? Poverty is making him pursue a version of the small wins strategy. A poor person has to become penny-wise in order to survive for the day. He has to do daily the mental arithmetic to best use the few dollars he has in hand. When he is in the grocery store walking by the racks, he is doing that every moment. The stress associated with this reduces the opportunities for him to do the 'pound-wise' calculations. And, he ends up pound-foolish: the perpetual and inescapable trap of poverty! Similar is the case with small wins.

The fact is that small wins mindset often do not favor big wins. Small wins just redirect your attention to easily achievable short term goals, while giving the illusory idea of progress. Since small wins are easily measurable, reward systems favor that approach, too. So, that is an added incentive for the management practitioners to implement this strategy.

The larger issue is, while big goals can indeed be decomposed into smaller goals, achievement of those smaller goals won't guarantee the achievement of bigger goals: you can dismantle a tall ladder into smaller segments and climb to the top step on each; evidently, even after climbing up on all the small ladders, you won't reach the peak where the undismantled ladder would have taken you.

When you apply this idea to innovations, it is easier to see that many incremental innovations necessarily do not equate with a single radical innovation. The original formulation of the small wins theory was a proposal to address social problems. Far fetching it as a management strategy might do more harm than good - especially when strategy in business is more of a design to pursue opportunities than a way to solve pre-existing problems.

Don't "Believe" in Evolution: Break its Code

No, I am not a creationist. The theory of evolution is no less credible than the theory of gravitation. What I am trying to say here is something different.

Evolution has made us to fit with the demands of the past, not of the present nor of the future. There is no magic in our body that predicts how the future might turn out to be and help our bodies to evolve in advance of the future challenges. If a particular kind of environment remains relatively stable for a period of time, certain species adapt to that environment and they survive its trying conditions. Our forefathers did adapt well to the conditions imposed upon them during the hunter-gatherer times. *That evolution however did make its deep imprints upon us and it has now begun to hurt us more than ever before.*

The hunter-gatherer times still provide us the frame of reference for our intuitions, intentions, behavior, and also happiness. Unfortunately, we are still trapped in a time period in our collective history that we left behind long back. This makes us vastly unprepared to deal with the demands of the future. It is as if the same evolutionary forces that help a species in one set of environmental conditions become its biggest hindrance to adapt to a different set of environmental conditions. The savior can transform into an annihilator, if the species doesn't realize this trap and *consciously* jump ahead of the curve of evolution.

We may not be able to alter the way evolutionary forces changed our anatomy for the hunter-gatherer times but, thankfully, we can reprogram our minds. We don't need to have a caveman's mind, while our physical brains still struggle with the inertia of 'evolutionary gradualism'. A situation might have caused a particular consequence for our ancestors: that does not mean a similar situation in the future would impact us similarly. Actually, studies like <u>THIS</u> show that intelligent people have successfully overcome the backward force of evolution: interestingly, for intelligent people, life satisfaction is built more around the current consequences of their situations than their ancestral consequences.

In general terms, our out-of-the-box mental ability to think of consequences uninfluenced by the evolutionary learning from the ancient past is what can make us evolve to adapt to the unforeseen challenges of the future. *In the history of human evolution, our minds evolved in consequence to the evolution of our bodies. Now, we are presented with the unique possibility to overcome the limitations of our bodily evolution with the powers of our mind.*

Unfollow, Unfriend, and Detox your Mental Life

Until recently in my life, I incessantly tried to entertain toxic people and their ideas. What's more, I felt it unbecoming of a healthy mind not to be open to such diversity. I consciously controlled my evolutionarily learned 'fight or flight syndrome' from kicking itself in - by detaching myself from the emotional contexts of arguments and by taking the stance of an independent observer.

May be I am getting too old too fast. Anyway, lately, I realized this had been taking a huge toll in terms of my peace of mind: so, I began to unfollow or even unfriend from my social networks some of the most poisonous of people and groups. I did not want to be rude to them, I just let them fade away from my life silently. If you strive for peace in life, this is a small step in the right direction, with a lasting positive impact. I can already feel the difference.

I do have a fetish for reason and I find true beauty in the application of logic with empathy. I can also entertain various harmless forms of irrationality - especially for the poetic beauty and truth contained in them. But, intelligent people who misconstrue arguments to support their preconceived conclusions are no longer welcome in my life. So also are irrational people who have pawned their brains to the aforesaid group and are carried away by their vested designs.

If you are one like me, try this. Get rid of toxicity before it grows in cancerous proportion.

The Rise of Knowltures, as Traditional Cultures Disappear

Knowlture (n): Unique cultural assumptions and practices emanated among the individual adherents of similar knowledge groups and professions.

The traditional definition of culture did include the component of knowledge in its definitional ambit. But, more than that, a cultural group is assumed to be formed based on its cumulative deposit of experience, beliefs, values, attitudes, meanings, *hierarchies,* religion, notions of time, roles, spatial relations, concepts of the universe, and possession of material objects. Say, a person could be Chinese, irrespective of whether he were a nano scientist, an opera artist, or a Foxconn factory laborer. According to various studies, primarily as a result of globalization and (information-communication) technological revolutions, bases of traditional cultural divides are increasingly being withered away. Many futurists have begun to proclaim that the world is now almost flat in terms of cultural differences.

What remains relatively unnoticed is the birth of various new kinds of *culture equivalents*, developed among groups of people engaged in different knowledge professions. I name them *knowltures* and these proliferate at staggering pace. Most knowltures, however, may have much shorter life cycles than traditional cultures.

As the available repertory of global knowledge doubles every year, our relative knowledge illiteracy - the number of people who do not have the understanding of a particular knowledge - also increases exponentially. Everyone of us might be knowing much more than our forefathers: but, each of us know a much smaller fraction of the available global knowledge than our forefathers during their lifetime (Google can bring you the information pertaining to a knowledge contour, but understanding the same is an entirely different game). As we spend more of our lives with people in our knowledge professions and interact mostly (only) with the systems and processes associated with these professions, birth of knowltures are inevitable.

The increase in knowltures in our society is likely to kill the anti-Malthusian promise of ephemeralization, a term coined by Buckminster Fuller, the ability of technological advancements to do more and more with less and less until

George, Babu P.

eventually we can do everything with nothing. The fundamental reason is, knowltures protect their self interests: *Knowledge-haves* will tend to protect their exclusive possessions and deprive *knowledge-have-nots* of the benefits of their knowledge. Thanks to knowletures, we humans have to postpone our utopian dreams once more.

The force of knowltures is already evident in the contemporary society. If all the revolutionary advancements in science and technology that we have had since mid 20th century failed to wipe out issues like poverty and malnutrition, the underlying reason is right here. Unfortunately, knowltures with superior knowledge possessions promote *knowledge racism*: while competition for necessities is not necessary anymore, such reincarnations of the human selfish gene ensures that we never reach our ideas. In a curious turn of events, our knowledge about other cultures helped us wipe off a great deal of traditionally held mutual misunderstandings; however, proliferation of knowledge and segregation of the same in professions also meant the creation of new cultural monsters.

Knowlture is the new face of culture. It is ugly but bold. It is here to linger and keep us dividing.

Now, you have a 'Scientific' Reason to Rationalize your Previous Unemployment

According to this study recently published in the American Sociological Review, doing a job that doesn't make optimal use of your knowledge, skills, and abilities can diminish your chances of future employment that require these KSAs. In other words, accepting 'some job' to survive during your periods of unemployment may make you unfit for reemployment in the category of the lost job. This could happen partially due to the actual erosion of KSAs as a result of their longer term non-use and partially due to the perception of future employers about the employability of the candidate. For example, think of an oil field engineer who lost his job recently accepting the job of a Walmart cashier. It is not hard to imagine how a couple of years on the new job will negatively impact his re-employability in the oil field.

So, is it a better idea to remain unemployed when you are laid off - until you get back a job comparable to the one lost? While the researcher who published the above paper has not considered all the negative consequences of unemployment, it is evident that periods of unemployment will create various other tolls upon people: unless there exist substantial savings, how will one pay for food, rent, healthcare, children's education, and a range of day to day expenses? If you are unlucky, significant unexpected expenses might surprise you, too. Loss of self-esteem could happen either way: people of different personality types may have different ways of perceiving it. For some, the loss of self esteem from doing a menial job may be more or less than that from remaining unemployed.

Some of my friends who are in the recruiting business says to "bury" the sub-par employment in discussions, if you feel morally obligated not to lie outright about it. They suggest not to use a chronological work history in the resume but rather highlight the most significant employment first. At least some employers do like the positive spirit of candidates - the willingness to do any job during hard times- and honestly mentioning what one did may not be all that bad at all. This, along with the mention of some credible volunteering work, may be all that one need for filling the gap. The typical armchair solution - go back to school and acquire further education - might work for some, too. Unfortunately, despite its quick appeal, there is not much credible research to prove that swimming against the tides and doing this will reward substantially in the near future.

Marketing's Success in the Commercialization of Human Self through the Social Media

Long back, Jean-Jacques Rousseau distinguished two kinds of self love. His coined the term a*mour-propre* to represent self esteem that depends upon the opinion of others. Rousseau contrasted it with *amour de soi*, which did not involve seeing oneself as others saw one. The global rise of self love in the form of a*mour-propre* is actually the dialectical product of purer forms of individualism and collectivism. It has certain key facets of both individualism (self) and collectivism (self as seen by the others), but is qualitatively different from these two.

I find beauty in the rise of the individual above the vulgarly generalized collective. It is a revolt against the subjugation of the human spirit, originally designed to be distinct and unique. If self love (more technically called, narscicism) would mean worshiping the self (e.g.: I love myself for who i am) rather than the image of the self as defined by others (e.g.: how many people like my social media posts), that is just great. If I don't love myself for who I am, who else will! However, unfortunately, only the latter kind of self love is growing faster; self love that is not unrelatable is being looked down upon and the room available for its nurture is gradually shrinking.

It is quite natural that people love to feel good about themselves, intrinsically, irrespective of the utility of the same for others. Alas, this has no marketing value; there is no benefit from individuals' intrinsic self love for the global advertisement industry, unless an individual's self love is a matter of concern for the others. In other words, (only) certain type of individual narscicism is a goldmine for commercial and other mind domination oriented forces.

The phenomenal success of social media platforms over the last decade is rooted in the synergization of these two apparent incompatibilities. Social media celebrate and promote those aspects of individual selves of their users that are of interest to others. Social media users are tricked to think that a*mour-propre* is*amour de soi* while also making it easier for global business interests to define, mass-customize, and social market *amour de soi* for everyone.

This way, individuals think they have a unique voice without them actually knowing that their voices just mirror the voices manufactured by the global elites. The process happens so naturally: I may think wearing that special kind of Nike sneaker is a reflection of my unique individual personality; I just don't know it mirrors the generalized interest carefully constructed for me by Nike. Such level of global success in commercializing the Self could be the greatest (and probably the ugliest!) marketing hack of the century.

My Second Childhood

At the peak of my craze to be loved by the world, I stopped knowing myself. With my desire to grow the way the world wanted me to become, I abandoned myself fully. In that frenzy, now I realize, I had neither me nor the world - except in those cleverly crafted illusions I am made to live by.

Thank goodness, I couldn't neglect forever the reverberations that kept drumming the walls of my heart from the suffocations of my soul. At one stage, I could afford my worldly illusions no longer - there was no more light at the end of the tunnel: In that hopelessness, hit the bounds of the simulacra hard, fell, bled, and broke down.

When all that I thought who I was shattered into pieces, I felt even worse. The succumbing thought that I have no more purpose, no more reason to continue to live, dropped in to fill the void created by the recess of the artificial. Then, very slowly, in that bare nakedness, I began to see glimpses of my true self revealing itself: that very innocent self from which I was made to drift away, ever since my childhood. When the dirt of all the falsehood that I thought I was made up of melted away, I saw once again, and felt for real, the purity, peace, and joy that I was.

With that came a unique opportunity, to give wings to my visions deeply preserved during all these lost years and to build further upon the authentic me that I met with, finally. Now I know: for me to become a better me, first I need to begin with who I am.

I am back on my journey, a journey that only I could do, once again. My second childhood.

Net Present Happiness: Can we Profitably Invest Present Happiness?

I use the term *Net Present Happiness* to mean the value, in the present terms, of a sum of happiness generated over future time periods, when the happiness actually available for consumption in the present is diverted for investment at a compound interest. In other words,

$$NPH = \sum \{Ht / (1+r)^t\} - Ho$$

NPH = Net present value of future happiness
Ht = Happiness generated during time 't'
r = discount rate of happiness
Ho = Present happiness sacrificed

In addition to a basic consideration for the time value of happiness that is sacrificed in the present, the discount rate should reflect the uncertainty of future happiness flows; the higher the uncertainty of future happiness flows, the greater should the discount rate be.

Now, the rule of thumb: *Don't invest your present happiness in any venture unless the net present value of your future happiness is more than the value of the present happiness thus invested.*

Even those of us who have never ever made financial investments routinely make happiness investments. However, we rarely think about the value of such investments in the present terms. As a result, many such investments will prove themselves to be wrong decisions. In the unidirectional flow of time, alas, we can only look back at our wrong investments and lament about them.

While unlike money happiness cannot be quantified, meditating upon the present sacrifices and their associated future benefits could still be helpful. We may even be able to generate subjectively meaningful numbers to represent each of these. Similarly, a discount rate could be proposed that matters to each one's particular life situation and based on how hedonistic or ascetic each one's overall happiness orientation is. From there, we could apply the formula and calculate NPH. Finally, before taking the decision to invest our present happiness in exchange of an uncertain future happiness, we may ask ourselves if that decision make us happy: the happiness associated with the decision to sacrifice the present happiness is at least good omen and a quick bonus.

At first, this exercise may seem impractical and unrealistic. True, decisions in life are so much more complicated than the most sophisticated of financial investment decisions. Let that not discourage you. I have made a few decisions recently, crudely applying this methodology. I know I may not remain alive to experience the longest term consequences of my decisions. But, what is important is that I can fathom the NPH of my decisions; this will at least make me feel content that the sacrifices made in the present are worth.

The many Benefits of not being so Positive in Life

I do not need to highlight the benefits of having a positive outlook: everyone knows those and businesses worth billions of dollars have sprouted around making people surrounded by positive fantasies. It is believed that positive thoughts inspire people to act upon their fantasized dreams and thereby create futures that embodies those dreams. The logic is simple, straightforward, and unquestionably convincing. Yes, (only) if you can dream, you can make it real.

However, recent research questions this dominant wisdom. For example, thisstudy published in *Psychological Science* indicates that being positive often means longer term depression. Positive thoughts did help to ease stress in the shorter term, however. I can understand why research studies like this are generally unappealing to folks: no doubt, there is an instant"feel good" about positive thinking. But, in good science, facts should not be traded for fantasies.

After reviewing the related literature, I have come to my tentative conclusion and it goes like this: *assuming we can feel the best happiness associated with an achievement by multiple kinds of efforts, we choose the least of those efforts that gets us the happiness.* Studies show that many a time people with sexual fantasies choose to masturbate rather than work harder to really have sex with their objects of fantasy. In this case, for them, real sex will involve elevated risks and sacrifices for any equivalent amount of happiness. If you are seeking an example for the other extreme, assume that one is interested in bowling. For the net equivalent amount of happiness, the relative effort required to drive to a nearby bowling alley and do the real bowling is much less compared to sit at home and daydream hard about bowling. Thus, you will stop daydreaming and instead choose to go to the bowling ally.

Another downside of much of positive thinking is that it implicitly assumes the present is dissatisfying. For you to visualize a better future, your mind concocts contrasts: one way to do that is to make you feel miserable in the present. So, this way, the benefits of positive thinking, even for the present and the short term, are somewhat questionable. Unfortunately, scholarly researchers have not investigated the topic of positive psychology as much as motivational gurus who are fixated on their pre-packaged solutions.

In this write up, I am not asking you to shed your healthy positive thoughts. To an extent, positive thoughts are important to inspire us, to make us feel and do good. Yet, beyond a point, fantasizing upon the positive can actually have the reverse outcome: it can make you uninspired, demotivated, and disconnected from the complex realities surrounding our lives.

It is in our best interest to learn to experience the crude beauty in being and living real. However, if this sounds too stoic and if you really crave for fantasies, try to *do it upon the outcome than upon the process*: constantly visualizing upon the joy of physical exercises in a gym may actually demotivate you from working out. It is much easier to get the net happiness that way: the imagined process of physical exercises in a gym is so much easier than the effort to be taken for that in a real gym (as often noted, people who constantly post on Facebook their daily exercise regimen are less likely to work out as much as their counterparts who don't).

How a Little Known Theory in Human Behavior Played out over Millions of People Overnight? Facebook's #SupportDigitalIndia Campaign in India.

On September 27, in the morning, Mark Zuckerberg, founder and CEO of Facebook Inc., changed his Facebook profile display picture (DP), apparently in support of Digital India, the Indian government's apparent effort to connect rural communities to the internet and give people access to more services online. It did not create any splutter or splash immediately. Mark had created for himself an unsavory image in India when he promoted his *internet.org* initiative: it was packaged as free internet but with the malicious intent of fundamentally thwarting the idea of net neutrality. Despite using Facebook as their primary means of social engagement, only very few could accept Facebook's support for a biased Internet, even when it was (ironically) packaged as "free internet".

However, by the evening, on the same day, Narendra Modi, the Prime Minister of India, followed suit with his own modi-fied DP. Modi, supported by world class PR experts and campaign managers, is probably one of the largest crowd pullers in the contemporary India. In no time, the followers (often called "bhakths") took charge of the job: millions of Indians applied the #supportdigitalindia filter to their own Facebook profile pictures; these changes took place at the amazing pace of a nuclear chain reaction.

George, Babu P.

"Co-Consumption": Introducing Co-Creation's Neglected Cousin

Co-creation is used in the marketing literature to refer to situations where stakeholders other than the producers, especially customers, become part of the production process. According to this, customers, instead of being passive recipients of value, are actively involved in the production of value that matter to them. Co-creation can be optional (like, a customer exercising his choice in buying a pre-configured Dell laptop or customizing specifications before ordering it) or compulsory (like, in the use of self-service technologies). Benefits for the co-creating customer could be both instrumental and experiential. Anyway, the stated objective of co-creation, primarily, is to maximize the value for the customer. Co-creation is a prominent figure in the Service Dominant Logic (SD-Logic), evolved in the early 2000's to understand services consumer behavior.

However, I would argue that the the SD-Logic will remain merely a flawed and imperfect Customer Dominant Logic (CD-Logic) unless we recognize co-creation's thus far neglected cousin, *co-consumption*. The reason is, co-creation presented only a partial perspective: that is, the perspective of the customer. The benefits to the customer fill all the pages of the co-creation literature. It neglects the equally important other party in encounters - the service provider. Traditionally, employees are considered to be internal customers. Yet, their costs or benefits are not equally weighed in the SD-Logic.

When the customers wish to *co-create*, employees wish to *co-consume*. As an example, in the classrooms, while the graduate students (customers) experience the co-create of knowledge, professors (service providers) experience the co-consumption of knowledge. Students who do projects, discover new knowledge, and present it in the classroom put themselves in the shoes of their professors; professors who listen to and learn from such student presentations put themselves in the shoes of their students. I would call this an 'inversion hypothesis' when the customers would seek to embrace the producer experience (co-creation) and the producer would seek to embrace the customer experience (co-consumption).

The SD Logic is perfected only if both these processes happen simultaneously, hand in hand. Customer sense of fulfillment from co-creation can reach optimal levels only with the corresponding service provider sense of fulfillment from co-

consumption. Yet, thanks to our skewed understanding that marketing is all about customers, service provider experiences from co-creation are not considered worthy of attention, in scholarly or in professional circles.

Actually, in many situations, employees actively seek out the opportunities for co-consumption. While carrying out a market research project recently, some of my students interviewed Russian nationals who come to Goa, India, and join as employees in various night clubs. One response that stood out was that their singular motive was to consume the experience of being tourists while assisting the tourists who frequent the night clubs. This motive was the key driver for them to perform optimally: their need to co-consume made them to invite the tourist customers to co-create experiences with them. Co-creation is the experience for the customers and co-consumption is the corresponding experience for the service providers.

The term 'co-consumption' is already used in various fields of inquiry to imply various things. But, there is an imperative need to associate this term with the experiences that service providers undergo in co-creation situations. To further this stream of research, we need collaboration from both consumer and organizational researchers.

You can't Reap the Moment you Sow: Latency Effect in Social Systems

In engineering terms, latency refers to the time interval between a stimulation (cause) and its response (effect). Latency is researched and documented extensively in the case of physical *systems*. However, in the case of social systems, it is not equally well understood. There exists only scant research aimed at conceptualizing and operationalizing it. Worse, decision makers are largely unaware of the existence of latency in the cause-effect relationships.

Imagine this. The CEO of a mediocre company takes some decision. In the short-to-medium term, his company experiences a severe downturn. The downturn is attributed to his decision and he is asked to leave. The next CEO is appointed who makes certain other decisions, apparently to reverse the fate of the company. In no time, the fortune of the company U-turns and the up-tide makes it one of the best players in the industry. In the fresh narrative, the up-tide is immediately attributed to the new CEO. He is rewarded abundantly and is declared a champion of the industry. In reality, this turns out to be a series of mis-attributions, all due to our skewed understanding of causes and how these causes are 'moved' to their effects.

In the scenario painted above, I am not talking about a CEO's actions resulting in better or worse outcomes as a result of favorable or unfavorable headwinds over which he has no control. Say, if a country's new tax policies or budgetary announcements may favor business operations in it, even an indifferent CEO might be able to show something good on the balance sheet. Likewise, even the best CEOs may not be able to show good results if some of the key environmental variables change for bad. Let me reiterate, these influences are different from the latency effect I discuss here.

The latency effect is about the time delay it takes for an action to result in its corresponding outcomes. It is not about the 'luck' factors that favor your actions. In the physical world, certain latency cannot be avoided due to the 'less than infinite' speed of light. The upper limits of latency are often material dependent (say, in communication, optical fibers offer much less latency than coaxial cables).

While latency is hard to measure in the human-social world, at least we should be able to anticipate a sense of it. Yet, there is no mention of it in most of our published causal studies. We have umpteen studies in consumer research establishing that 'customer satisfaction determines loyalty' and 'service quality determines customer satisfaction'. But, almost none of these studies say "*it takes 'x'-units of time for the effect to propagate*" or "*there is 'p' probability that it takes 'x'-units of time for the effect to propagate*". So, effectively, we know $y=f(x)$ but not whether it will happen in a second or in a hundred years.

More research is needed to perfect a methodology to measure latency in social systems. Agreeing that there is no perfect(ed) method right now, in carefully planned longitudinal observational studies, we can get some idea of the latency fairly easily. In questionnaire based surveys, we can include relevant item statements to gather latency related data (although subjective and opinionated). In many situations, relevant secondary data can help, too.

Some knowledge of the expected latency is critically important in the evaluation of managerial and policy interventions; in the absence of it, we only have flawed ideas of causes and effects. Obviously, it is not fair. Less obviously but more importantly, it is not an effective strategy.

Fabricated Scientific Disciplines and Fictitious Growth of Science

Is canonizing a new saint to Christianity going to make it a better religion? Will eliminating one saint make it any worse?

The pace of introduction of new constructs (concepts salted with additional layers of abstractions) is widely considered to be a key measure of the vibrancy of a field of inquiry. Every field of inquiry is a network of constructs. If a new observed phenomenon in the scope of it cannot be explained as a relationship among the existing constructs ("gap in the literature"), new constructs are explored, identified, and introduced. The 'nomological network' of constructs and their relationships proliferate over time; there will reach a stage when a field of inquiry can confidently address almost every new problem in its ken without the help of additional constructs. Yes, a young area of inquiry has thus become a mature discipline!

Now, there is this problem. What will the establishment do? In particular, what will those who were accustomed to finding a means of living in that field of inquiry do? Will they settle themselves to the role of teachers who merely share the saturated wisdom already there? No. They understand that uninterrupted new knowledge discovery is critically important for their survival as a privileged class. Thus, when there is no more new knowledge to be discovered in a discipline, they will start inventing knowledge.

The commonest manner by which knowledge is invented in a discipline is by means of the introduction of newer constructs (at times, some of the extant constructs are made to retire, too). Entire breeds of PhD students do their research projects solely with the objective of fabricating constructs and then rationalizing their relevance and importance. Along the lance, these artificial constructs will generate additional 'theoretical' problems for further investigations. As a chain reaction, newer constructs and associations are proposed. Lo, the discipline is on a fully contained self-propulsion mode now!

While the aforesaid deterioration is common across disciplines, social sciences are particularly prone to it (Physical-chemical-biological sciences always have some or the other new 'real' problems and genuinely serious researchers are rarely faced with the pressure to fabricate. Mathematicians may invent entirely new nomological worlds out of thin air, but seeking mathematical truth is purposeful beyond the self-constructed boundaries of its discipline).

Coming back to the question I posed at the beginning of this article, it is not hard to see the semblance. In a matured religion, a new saint is introduced not to explain an unexplained miracle; rather, miracles are sought from pillar to post, in order to justify the induction of someone into sainthood. If there was no intention to ordain a new saint, any and all of these miracles could easily have been attributed to some of the existing saints. Anyhow, once someone becomes a saint, new miracles will begin to appear in their name, further fortifying their position in the network.

Can Christianity sustain itself without any more saints? Or, better, let us ask, can a scientific discipline sustain itself without any more constructs? I must conclude, there is a stage at which the processes in science go quite parallel with those in religion.

Should our Schools Reward the Disciplined but Punish the Intelligent?

If self-discipline is the primary objective of education, how are our schools different from jails?

SCHOOL
. authoritarian structure
. dress code
. emphasis on silence and order
. negative reinforcement
. walk in lines
. loss of individual autonomy
. abridged freedoms
. no input in decision making
. set times enforced for
  walking, eating etc.

PRISON
. authoritarian structure
. dress code
. emphasis on silence and order
. negative reinforcement
. walk in lines
. loss of individual autonomy
. abridged freedoms
. no input in decision making
. set times enforced for
  walking, eating etc.

You may ask, from where I got the idea that schools reward self-discipline over intelligence. Well, it has always been a topic in the debates on education. There is no scarcity of credible primary research supporting this view, too. See for instance Duckworth, and Seligman (2005): these researchers from the University of Pennsylvania conclude beyond doubt that self-discipline outdoes IQ in predicting the academic performance of the adolescents.

Numerous studies indicate that intelligent people are less likely to be obedient, disciplined, and hardworking (although lack of intelligence in someone doesn't mean he is hardworking). Consequently, the school system is not just neutral to the intelligent, but also punish them severely. If a less intelligent student who works in a systematic and focused way to grasp the course materials is more likely to earn straight A's than his more intelligent but less disciplined counterpart, it is both a curse upon the intelligent and an absolute indictment against mankind's intellectual progress.

You may find merit in self-discipline based education. It is not hard to see how the current system aids everyone having a work life (a job, a living!) as long as they are motivated to work hard, following a prescription. Fundamentally, the system has industrialized education: as a result, it is best suited for knowledge sharing to the largest number of people in the most efficient manner. It minimizes much of the 'undue advantage' that some people have because of their natural but unearned (a.k.a. not the result of their effort) endowment called intelligence. It also recognizes the fact that it is not as easy to develop intelligence as it is to train in knowledge and skills.

The damage done is likely to exceed any benefit, though. Given their stress on consistence and persistence, schools kill nonstandard behavior. It stifles the inspiration to be curious and kills creativity. It prioritizes static stability over dynamic equilibrium.

Given their polar opposite positions, educating intelligence and discipline simultaneously for the masses is almost impossible. That said, as a common fact, we all are wired to discover patterns and principles. Our school system could help the students to engage this raw intelligence more, the natural desire of every man to understand, apply, and extend. Even children with relatively low intelligence can vastly improve their intelligence when their schools focus more on making them think what to do with knowledge than to reward them for amassing more and more knowledge.

If our schools cannot teach intelligence, they lose all their noble standing. There is nothing more exalted or reverential about them. They are no longer our lofty laboratories where we experiment with the roots of our futures. Should the most valuable lesson that our children learn in the schools is the primacy of self-discipline and hard work? I disagree.

That Magical Question which (Dis)solves all your Problems

Sometimes, when you are overburdened with the weight of a multitude of troubling questions, a fairy might appear in front of you and ask you just one more question. A question that can make you momentarily spellbound. Your answer to this latest question will be simple and straightforward enough. That answer will also simultaneously solve all your other problems. How enchanting!

It is as if all the solutions were ripe and ready waiting to reveal themselves but for the appearance of this magical question; it is as if all these questions were to be raised first before answering any single one of them; and, it is as if the final revealing question has no particular meaning until all the preceding questions are asked.

Think of this simple example: imagine you are troubled by a number of questions like 'whether people love me', 'what others think of me', 'am I being loved or hated for who I am', etc? Then, sooner or later, an interesting question might pop up in your mind: 'why should I bother myself with what others think of me?'. That reflective question, I believe, is capable of dis(solving) all the other previous questions that kept afflicting you all along.

How often did you have similar experiences? During their investigations, philosophers and scientists encounter this pattern all the time. We common folks find it more often while trying to solve various puzzle filled games. Say, it is almost impossible to win a good game of chess until you are burdened with this pattern first. To be fair, we are not particularly conscious of this pattern even as it emerges frequently in the background of our mental processing.

To prepare the ground for the finishing game is not an effort wasted. However, with solutions not visible right before our naked eyes, we may decide to quit prematurely. While trying to tackle complex problems, it will be helpful to recognize and be mindful of the invisible emergence of this pattern in the background. We must realize that solutions are often interconnected and that solutions to particular problems cannot come about without first raising a series of other (seemingly unrelated) problems.

It might take a lot of time (and luck!) for your sole brain to brew up all these questions all by itself. This is not particularly efficient and effective, too. The pattern development process can be accelerated by brains working together.

Also, it need not be a magical visitor coming from elsewhere to raise that critically important revealing question: it could appear in a rusted creative corner of your own brain or that of an equally burdened co-worker. So, do mindfully watch out for that path-braking *serendipity question*!

A Generation of 'Unpredictable People': Marketing to Moving Targets

It was probably easier for you to answer the question "who are you?" a couple of decades back than it is today. Not only was it easier to answer but also the answers had longer term temporal reliability. Even if we manage to give an answer to this question today, we are unsure how long we will hold on to it. We are increasingly men in the making, *human identities of possibility*. Such identities are not shifting continuously either; rather, this process is marked by a sense of discontinuous time. We are a-historical and the values of our past generations cannot be identified by iterating back historically.

The contemporary man does not have something definite and lifelong at the center of his soul. Multiple personalities float within us, each take birth, live, and die quite sporadically. We want to be everything but at the same time be different from everything. In our journeys, we have the company of everyone but not the lifelong company of anyone. With no significant increase in lifespan, we crave to absorb way more sensations than people who lived before us - which also means we abandon some of these sensations on the way.

Our uncertainty about the truth value of things, which include scientific facts, is one reason we are less committed to them; more manifestly, it is our generation's indomitable desire to escape from monotony, boredom, and unidimensionality (push motivator) and the corresponding opportunities for limitless alternate experiences (pull motivator). We don't actually care if these experiences are real or simulated. The very idea of lifelong commitment to anything - be it products, ideas, or relationships - is increasingly becoming alien to us. Written contracts still largely stay, but hearts move on.

Since the present day man is gifted with an umpteen array of choices but has got only limited time on earth as noted above, he has no leisure time before hopping from choice to choice; he has to get into the deepest trenches of each experience quickly and get gratification instantly. Yet, his deep emotional commitment to anything that he clamps his heart on is a very genuine kind of loyalty. It is authentically sincere and deeply felt, but it lasts only for a wink span of time. For the market researcher, this realization is inescapable: if a test-retest reliability analysis of the longitudinal findings related to consumer behavior is performed, inconsistencies are hard to miss.

Thus, is this the end of marketing theory as we know it? What is the future of marketing practice built on the ideas of stable customer segments and targeting these segments? My friends in the market research profession often quip the futility of classifying consumers into well defined and lasting segments. You may know some people who possess an old fashioned Nokia phone that they use as a reliable partner during their camping trips, a gold plated iPhone matching their lifestyle aspirations, and a Blackberry for business communications. While there is a space for every kind of phone for these people, the aforesaid usage pattern might evaporate tomorrow as if it never was the case. Should we invest millions and spend years to (try to) understand the behavior of people if such behavior is already known to be so chaotic?

I believe the blueprint of New Marketing should be built on the understanding that everyone is your potential customer and that whether someone becomes your actual customers or not depends largely upon a range of contingency factors. Marketing should not exclude consumers with certain personality types forever, as if they are irrelevant. You can sell anything to anyone by knowing the coordinates upon which their instantaneous existences are anchored. So, knowing this, that is the emerging role of market research.

We do that already to some extent when the internet users are presented with personally targeted advertisements in accordance with what each of them feel at a moment as captured in terms of their online behavior and triangulated with various other corroboratory evidences. Also, marketing's failure to identify long lasting behavioral patterns does not mean that it cannot concoct sensational spikes in consumers. Experience has demonstrated that marketing interventions are effective in configuring the behavioral shifts in a desired manner in the short term. Then, marketing success is all about catering to the sensational requirements of these configurations instantly with matching products and services. Advances in information-communication technologies and physical distribution systems make it to leverage this possibility easier than ever.

In Praise of Plagiarism

After spending more than fifteen years in the academic research profession, I am slowly coming to the realization that the term plagiarism contains way more smoke than fire. While taking credits for someone else's work is clearly unethical and is to be duly punished, what the anti-plagiarism enforcement squad typically achieves is overly useless and often counter-intentional.

First, the futility factor. Imagine, an academic scholar of marketing came out with the revelation (in the form of a scholarly publication) that 'word of mouth' publicity has a significantly better impact in the collective cultures than in the individualistic ones. Anti-plagiarism enforcement regimes typically examine only whether other authors (or, even the very same author!) have copied and pasted this finding in their research papers without citing the original author. It does not bother itself with the equally or more important question of whether practicing businesses exploit this idea to their advantage without giving credits to the aforesaid original author. Anyway, when was the last time a business cited an academic author as it implemented a finding from a research publication! (Patents and copyrights are rewarded, but not knowledge published in research papers). Evidently, we are not hitting where the nail is.

What motivated humans to investigate the secrets of nature and society long before the invention of the modern scholarly publishing machine? There is something inherently attractive in the search for knowledge. Will genuine researchers stop inquiry and have any less craving for research if plagiarists go unpunished? No, there is an iota of evidence to believe so. While others acknowledging one's contributions is a pleasing factor, great inventors and innovators are motivated by forces so much more fundamental than extrinsic reward systems.

The citation convention that we practice has its origins in the European universities rooted in western individualism: its spread across the world has brought in a fundamental change in perspective about the ownership of knowledge in many collective societies. Generations of students and scholars from these collective societies are still clueless about the value in citing others' works. I have had many Indian, Chinese, and Korean research students who failed to understand the purpose of citations: for them, knowledge is and is to be in the public realm; an individual researcher who invents or discovers something is just an agent of destiny and has to have no special privilege over it (these students don't claim ideas as their own; it is just that they don't consider it vital to attribute these ideas to other individuals). Ultimately, you did not work hard to design your brain structure!

The only remaining benefit of anti-plagiarism movement is in acknowledging the impact of co-researchers within the community of academic researchers. It offers a way to quantify research impact within the community. Even on this front, its benefit is questionable. Citation rackets are rampant. Also, citation is seen as an uninspiring toil and it is not uncommon for researchers to regurgitate others' ideas and avoid citing them. Worse, they are at times forced by unscrupulous journal editors and reviewers to find published sources even for the authors' own original yet to be published ideas. Likewise, policing self-plagiarism in the published content supports the academic publishing industry more than anyone else.

Thus, the requirement to cite each and every bit of previous knowledge, even the trivial ones, is at best a waste of effort. Also, this expectation (while it ensures that you 'stand on the shoulders of the giants before you') can forestall the acceptance of radically disruptive knowledge that does not fit with the current dominant design. Remember, wrongly accepted hypotheses can get perpetual lives by means of citations.

Fix Others Before Fixing Yourself. Yes, I Mean it!

"Clean up the mess in your own house before cleaning up the world": this seemingly innocuous and well meaning advice has harmed the world way more than you could possibly imagine.

It is deceptively stupid but damn dangerous. Remember, you heard it from parents while you were kids, heard it from teachers while you were in the school, and later heard it from spouse while you were married. You also hear various versions of it as the sayings of great men: Like, "you hypocrite, first take the plank out of your own eye ..." and "fix yourself before fixing others".

Remember how much of the mighty steam of your youthful idealism got evaporated instantly as each time you heard these advises since when you were a kid? We all have personal deficiencies and inadequacies: we are warned to address these first, become role models in our own lives, before going to change others and the world at large. Ultimately, we reconcile to that part of the advise which says "before fixing them" but fail to act on "fix yourself first". We come to accept the 'fact' that the world is unfair and then justify our own personal unfairness.

There is no rational basis to think that a person making his own personal life better will make the world better. It is a fallacious intuition at its best. Even if two by third of the people living in the world manages to do that, there is no guarantee for utopia. Again, it is insurmountably hard for anyone to even remotely do that, living in an unfair society. The chicken comes first: a good society is the starting point.

A jail cannot become a better ecosystem by a few individual prisoners cleaning up themselves in their personal lives; rather, if these same few inmates have a dream about how a healthy jail ecosystem should be and if they act for that, even the unruliest inmate in that jail will be healed along the way. The beauty of this is that not every inmate needs to have the idealism to clean up the whole. It is only that self-righteous authority figures don't moralize them to reform themselves first. Let us not bother them about their personal ethics, for the larger good.

Actually, the economist and social thinker in me says that if each of us take just a tenth of the effort we would take to clean up ourselves to reform the world, life for everyone will become so much more wonderful. Numerous scientific studies prove that people who live in good communities get transformed for good, notwithstanding their personal efforts to reform their personal lives (I am not advocating bad conduct here: it could be coincidental, but the personal lives of many great social change leaders were probably not filled with so much of goodness - may be they didn't want to wait to first make their homesteads clean before getting into the larger arena).

It works this way: a few overcome the self imposed boundaries of personal failings about themselves, work to make the society for good, and then goodness shall slowly prevail everywhere. It is far more easier for goodness to trickle down from the top (society) to the bottom (individual). If the society in which you live is good, you will most likely become good; your children will be born to a good society and they will grow up good, too.

Kettling in the Workplace: Provoke 'em as a Pretense to Terminate 'em.

Kettling is a crowd control method widely used during protest demonstrations. Police officers surround the crowd from all directions and then jam them to a very narrow area with very limited options to exit the cordon. The general intent is that this will minimize nuisance to the public not participating the protests. However, some social psychologists as well as conspiracy theorists view the use of kettling as a context cleverly constructed by the police to justify consequent retaliatory action.

The kettle metaphor is quite fitting: it relates the containment of protesters to the containment of water within a domestic kettle. Inherently, we humans don't want to be caged against our will and caging will burn our emotions up. In law enforcement contexts, typically, people heated up with rage will try to attack the police and engage in various other kinds of criminal activities (Once heated up, the water molecules have no way but to whistle up and escape from the kettle). No mention, attacking peace keepers is more than sufficient a justification for the use of brute force.

My discussion here, however, is related to a similar tactic adopted by business organizations. Over the last several years, I have interviewed many individuals who lost their jobs as a result of conditions that were carefully planted with a view to justify their terminations later. If you are an undesirable employee who needs to be terminated somehow and if there is no legitimate and rationally sound basis to punish you, kettling comes to help.

Often, the use of kettling is orchestrated by your boss with or without the connivance of significant others inside the organization. Unlike the more widely discussed cases of workplace harassment, the individual activities related to kettling are by themselves not strictly illegal. Say, you could be pressurized with odd shifts, too little or too much work, or by various kinds of subliminal blame games. You contain everything to yourself for a while but explode one day, quite in line with the script that they have prepared for you.

The beauty of this tactic is that the person who is at the receiving end will soon develop guilt feelings. Self attribution bias will kick in: everything the employer did to you will be buried deep down in your moral compass because those provocations were small and subliminal while what you did in consequence was quick, drastic, and in explosive proportion. Also, the ex-employer has by now important tangible evidences against you. Thus, you won't think of suing nor you can.

Sometimes, kettling can affect a group of employees. If you are unfortunate, even if you are merely a bystander, you could get kettled just because of your accidental relationships with the target group. It is not always easy to sense kettling in the workplace, especially in the early stages of being cordoned off.Noticing subtle changes in personal interactions require a good amount of emotional intelligence.

It is relatively easier to feel kettling if an entire group of employees is being kettled - provided there is an active communication mechanism among its members that will help them share significant cues. What it takes then is putting the pieces of the puzzle together. Yet, be-warned: the affected groups may have a tendency to inflate the perceived threat level and over-react.

Once you know you are being kettled, attempt to understand the underlying reasons. Inquire if there are mis-perceptions about your work or other aspects of life. If yes, try to correct these by engaging constructively with those who kettle you. You also have to begin to document all of your work related activities and communications. This will help you build a case for yourself later. Finally, be mindful of your propensity to self-blame and don't let yourself fall into that trap.

George, Babu P.

When Resistance to Change becomes Innovation: Or, Retrovation

Read a thousand scholarly pieces on innovation and, I can assure you, all of them will have at least one common recipe for successful innovation: *change*. Yes, an innovator is a change agent and those who resist change are doomed for hell. Vision, the push factor of innovation, is all about creatively destroying the present and leading change. Innovation means unfreezing the status quo, herding the masses to the future position which the vision dictates, and refreezing their tastes there. And, there is no dearth of innovations that fits this scheme.

However, in the dominant logic mentioned above, we sidestep an important class of innovations. I will call it *retrovation* and its champions retrovators. Retrovators are *retroverts* who see the mainstream society drifting in directions (often inspired by the promises of innovations) that they feel undesirable and resist such drifts. At times, they themselves would have moved along with these drifts for a while, before realizing the falsehood in the promises. Then, they retrovate by reverting the changes.

Once such realization settles in, it is a detour back home - to that better world that once existed and left behind. The call of retrovators include inspiring others who feel the same vacuum to go back and reconstruct the old conditions, products, and services. Unlike what the literature informs us, thus, conditions for innovation can prevail not only when the innovators move *faster* than the rest but also when they move significantly *slower or in a direction opposite to* the generalized direction of material development.

Monsanto is arguably an innovator, promising the dream of a genetically modified future. The world at large has sung to their tunes. Governments and farming entrepreneurs around the world saw their grand promises and moved along with them. Monsanto keeps revolutionizing the agricultural landscape of the world. Yet, a minority of 'anti-progressive' elements in the society saw the dangers inherent in it and called for a retro-revolution. Going back to the good old days, the times when we did organic, fertilizer free, small scale community farming, was one such solution proposed by these retroverts.

Every time I visit my home village in Kerala, India, I see many such retrovert farmers. Burgeoning incidents of cancer and other chemically induced diseases were an immediate trigger for the resurrection of these retroverts; but, they also nostalgically missed the pure beauty of the agrarian culture that bid them adieu when they turned to industrial farming. Chakkappan, my ninety year old grandfather, who still does farming, opened his heart up in front of me recently: it took for him decades to understand the wrong direction he was taken by the productivity-efficiency narrative of 'scientific farming'. Many young and educated members in the rural communities around the world are now vocally against Monsanto-like innovations.

Retrovation is visible in every industry, both in the arts and the scientific professions. People in large numbers want to stay away from many things that are deemed to be progressive. A friend of mine who runs rural tourism business in India doesn't offer anything other than modest huts, village cuisine, and rural sightseeing; he charges tourists more than what typical five star properties could. Healthy living is back in fashion. Bicycles and walking are popular again. Many app developers successfully market smartphone apps that are aimed at helping users overcome their technology addiction. Research upon what we did better in the past has proliferated, leading to phases of retro-revolution.

No doubt all these created a lot of noise and quackery (e.g.: retro filters are applied to images captured on advanced digital cameras, just for an imagined feel of the past); yet, the overall trend has been very promising. Not every development is progress and not every kind of progress is good for us. Mankind may indeed be heading for an ultimate extinction, but retrovations offer some hope.

George, Babu P.

'Just-in-Time Capitalism' and a New Era of Slavery

The operations management approach named 'Just-in-Time' never lost popularity since the Japanese businesses inaugurated it in the 1950's. However, until quite recently, its footprints were largely restricted to material inventory management in the manufacturing settings.

At its core, Just in Time (JIT) is a fairly simple idea: storage of unused inventory incurs a significant cost; hence, organize manufacturing in such a way that storage is minimized. While workers engaged in the manufacturing process had to readjust themselves to its efficiency expectations, JIT system in general did not consider workers as an inventory item. Mind it, that was not because of any lofty ideals about the human element. In fact, JIT systems until recently were incapable of effectively considering workers as variable costs, thanks to forecasting limitations about worker demands.

Things are changing fast. Just in time systems are not restricted to manufacturing processes or its workers anymore. Driven by the new 'data revolution', service industries are JIT's new crowned champions. Even traditionally, employment in the service industries had the inherent characteristic of uncertainty. That uncertainty has escalated to a new level because service employers can now fairly accurately predict the demand for their workers - just in time.

For instance, it is not uncommon these days that service employees are initially given only tentative work schedules the statuses of which keep changing until it is a few minutes before the actual work begins. Evidently, this is every capitalist's wet dream. It can phenomenally increase business profits and also, correspondingly, macro indicators of the 'health' of the national economy, like the GDP. Yet, the increased ability of businesses to predict the future demand for their products has correspondingly increased the unpredictability in the lives of their employees.

Ironical but true, *employer's certainty is employees' uncertainty*. Improvements in human resource management like this would have been nicer if the employees could practice JIT in their own lives. Instability resulting from the reduction in work hours and lingering uncertainty in the work schedules will quickly mirror in our personal lives as well. Yet, you cannot often treat personal lives just in time: even as your employer can deny you wages as a result of their last minute adjustments, daycare centers don't accept your children just in time on prorated fees; you still have to pay flat premiums for your healthcare and flat monthly rentals for a roof to live in.

Or, with services like Uber in increasing popularity, are we all finally adjusting to the just in time lifestyle implied by the cultural logic of this latest stage of capitalism? Interestingly, this new lifestyle is presented as freedom: freedom to consume without the burdens of ownership, freedom to collage apparently discreet elements of life and create novel experiences. Yet, not many realize the slavery that this new kind of freedom subsumes.

It may not be easy to fight against the mega winds or win over it. Also, the new system is bad not because the businesses increase their profits but because the employees, especially the lower rung workers, bear most of its burden. The solution, thus, could be in our political system rising to the times and institute safety nets in proportion to the increasing uncertainty arising in our work lives. Will it? Or, will we have the collective will to make it stand for us and do it?

Why am I on Facebook, Twitter, and LinkedIn? Some Unpleasant Truths.

Why? The simple answer, for most of us, in most situations, is: impress others of our positive highlights and airbrushes. If such highlights are nonexistent, we photoshop our personalities and material artifacts to bring the nonexistent into existence. Even when we post negative highlights, that is with a view to project positive perspectives of them.

We know what we post is not our real lives but rather the lives we wish others to see. Will posting so make our wishes any closer to reality? No. But, it gives us consolation prices when others 'like' our wishes. According to the intensity of likes and supportive comments, even though delusionally, we begin to feel the boundaries between the real and the wishful blurry and permeable. When you post on Facebook a photo that you have taken with a celebrity and when it gets enough likes, you feel closer to that celebrity than if you had to merely see the photo for yourself. Real pleasures and pains both lose their original sources of meaning; real meanings are rather reconstructed in the shared imaginations of those who like and comment on the posts.

The moment you stop looking at an enchanting natural scenery with your naked eyes and begin to look at it via the camera lens, some authenticity is lost. Still, the root is essentially preserved. However, when a photograph that you shot is shared on a social network and when your commentators take charge of interpreting it, you and your audience both begin to see a new reality underpinning that photo. That new reality is rooted entirely in the shared imaginations of the folk liking and commenting and need not necessarily have any correspondence at all with the original roots of its authenticity. The primary bias here is that this new perception is artificial; the secondary bias is that it is artificially *sweetened*.

So, are our social networks really making us us all happy? Do they give at least some global '*net fictitious happiness*'? No, a net fictitious happiness is highly unlikely. A group of people seeing a positively framed status update on your timeline and liking it does not mean that they feel happier seeing it. Many recent studies indicate that they rather begin to compare their actual (gloom) situation with your imagined (glee) situation and this comparison will make them feel miserable and vulnerable. In order to convince themselves and others that they have not lost out in the race, they do what you just did - of course with their own versions of concocted realities. Again, you and many others will like those posts. This effectively provides a fertile condition for the vicious cycles of negativity to spiral, camouflaged in the virtuous cycles of happiness. Yet, social media derived depressions and suicidal thoughts are underrepresented, thanks to our media's innate bias for the positive.

I shall make this statement in bold: *no one who is happy with their present selves, content with who they presently are, will be on a social network. Not even those who wish to merely communicate to the society who they really are.*

The fact that I am posting these thoughts on social media and that I am an active member on many popular social networks is certainly ironical. May be, such ironies characterize our complex existences in a socially constructed world, of which we can only deliberate, but from which we have little escape.

George, Babu P.

When More Media is Less Message: Or, Braess's Paradox in Communication

Last week, while addressing the organizational communication issues in a business unit that I am consulting for, I found myself stuck and clueless. The original complaint of the vast majority of employees of this business unit was that there was not enough communication from the top management. Based on employee feedback, it was decided to increase the deployment of a wide range of communication tools, especially the social media. That was in 2011.

Everyone was seemingly excited. In the new scheme, any employee could directly email the CEO and the VPs; in fact, anyone could communicate with everyone else directly, using a variety of electronic tools. Free, open, layer-stripping, and all-pervasive communication. All good, white as snow?

No, there was a new problem. May be, that is why I was invited to look into it. The problem the management faced was that increased media use actually made the original situation so much worse.

After sitting on this problem for a while, something very special attracted my attention. As a result of the new communication policy, words, pixels, and sound bytes were flying all around. The same messages were delivered via emails, chats, texts, tweets, and podcasts. Conversation was fun and it was nothing short of a crime not to join the chats. In no time, the depth of communication gave way for its breadth; the democratization of communication entirely took its relevancy away; increased communication frequency and variety led to decreased communication quality and utility. In the worst of ironies, no one began to take others seriously.

The provision of additional media options soon generated its own induced demand and people began to spend more time in the act of communicating. Increased efficiency of a resource like the media should ideally be decreasing our dependence upon it. More ink-efficient pens should mean that the quantity of ink demanded become lower. Yet, it did not happen that way. In other words,

Day after day, day after day, We stuck, nor breath nor motion;

As idle as a painted ship, Upon a painted ocean.

Words, words, every where, And all the boards did shrink;

Words, words, every where, Nor a syllable to make sense of.

Now, the employees change their minds again and blame the change leaders for their latest torments as well. Just like the crew that forces the *ancient mariner* to wear the dead albatross about his neck. The mariner cannot perform its coordinating functions effectively, either. But, the root cause somehow is escaping everyone.

The root cause of this situation is probably an extension of the Braess's Paradox. I learned it in my Network theory course as an undergraduate student. In essence, it demolishes the intuitive argument that adding more capacity to a transportation network would increase its efficiency. We build more roads to ease congestion. Yet, traffic management experiments have time and again demonstrated that the overall efficiency of the system is often improved when we close down some of the existing roads than by constructing more roads.

Can't this be true for communication media redundancy as well? In any case, the consulting solution I am going to give will be informed by my faith in it. While more media has certain unquestionable benefits, I need to find a way to 'tax away' its rebound effects.

Reimagining Community Based Education

Long back, community centered education was the only kind of education we had. Different ancient communities developed their own indigenous systems of education, each reflective of the aspirations of those societies (e.g.: the Indian gurukulas, the Greek gymnasiums, etc). Then, with the birth of modern universities, education became more and more 'universal': the university system stressed upon the development and dissemination of community-invariant, 'objective', universal knowledge often sidelining the nuanced aspirations of the communities within which they were physically located.

The ideological locations of 'progressive' modern universities needed not have a correspondence with their spacio-temporal locations: for example, Oxford University was physically located in Oxford but its connection with the locale largely ended there. True education should be to elevate human souls from the phenomenal world of immediate perceptions, for which campuses were to be isolated from local cultures and their values. For the good part, positivism of this kind resulted in the development of many world class institutions of learning and, associated with it, a globally shared human consciousness.

Yet, the usefulness for communities that nurtured educational institutions with a legion of graduates who cannot act locally was questioned by educational thinkers. Towards the early 21st century, this latter viewpoint gained significant traction. Ironically, it was globalization that made most of us realize the importance of going back to the local and the unique.

Even affirmative action programs like reserving certain percentage of seats for the local students were noticed to have unintended counterproductive effects. College educated students (and even those qualified in vocational trade schools) almost always left their communities after their graduation to pursue their dreams elsewhere: in many underdeveloped countries, the only benefit of supporting such higher education was that these graduates would pump back some of their savings 'to invest' in their native communities even as their brains and bodies toiled for masters elsewhere.

Most schools and colleges now have community extension divisions and programs. However, to be fair, these programs were not designed bottom up but were attempts to transplant the universalized knowledge held in the academic world to these communities. Communities were treated like novice students who did not know where they wanted to go and academic experts with their missionary zeal proselytized the community members - in vein.

In parallel, various non-academic nonprofits emerged in these communities who offered a new paradigm for community based development. Many of them had genuine intents and were supported by local governments and other community interest groups. In multiple ways, these nonprofits assessed community resources and matched them with opportunities. They developed capacity building programs for the local youth. However, these agencies at their best could provide the local community members only with short term vocational paths. Even their sincerest efforts were limited because of their sheer disconnect with the global issues and challenges to which local developmental priorities should be integrated in order to derive long term sustainable outcomes.

So, now that we have in front of us the deficiencies of these two extreme models of community based education, what is the way forward? I believe the way is to institute a coordinating-facilitating agency in each community that intersects with both the models. Such an agency should embrace the beneficial elements of both to inspire globally informed local action. It should propose evidence driven plans and course corrections for educational upliftment. For this to happen, it has to become a constantly updated, centralized, data bank about the community's educational situation. Nothing like a comprehensive information pool has the power to influence people to act; and, more so to commit them to own the consequences of their actions.

Information gathered from different kinds of educational programs and organizations will empower the coordinating agency to craft a shared vision for the community for which it stands. Shared vision is a significant catalyst of effective community based action in the right direction. Shared vision can weed out inefficiencies resulting from multiple agencies repeating the same thing, too. While building a seamless information architecture is key, equally important is that information available has to be interpreted with the community context as primary the frame of reference. That way, this agency will be rightly poised to offer 'situated wisdom' for its stakeholders groups.

Our Obsession with the Clock and Loss of Beauty in Life

Our experience of time-warping can be *calming* (e.g.: while listening to a very soothing sonata) or *throbbing* (e.g.: while skydiving, especially during the moments immediately preceding and succeeding the launch from the aircraft). In the calming situations, we feel that the rate of change of time has approached zero while in the throbbing situations we feel time is paced close to infinity. In fact, our minds actively seek out a blend of *time shrinking* and *time stretching*experiences and affording the quest of mind for such variety is at the heart of a truly rewarding life. Different individuals may have different innate preferences for calming or throbbing experiences and it is up to each one of us to recognize such differences and respond to their calls.

However, our obsession with the clock, the linear and impersonal time that the clock implies, has become an critical barrier to our experience of freedom, peace, and joy in life. The clock is a wonder machine that helps us plan our lives forward and is at the center of all the promises of our scientifically structured modern life; yet, it treats time as a person-experience invariant reality out there and imposes artificial structures upon some of our deeply personal time-evasive experiences. Given the myriad benefits of the clock in our modern lives, I will be the last one to demand dumping it down. What I advocate rather is that we scale down its permeance in those affairs that matter utmost to our souls. But, how do we exercise this 'middle way' solution?

The idea is to let time become 'the space' that our experiences choose to spread themselves to. Imagine going for a nature walk: don't provision a clock-ridden time segment for the same but let your experience of fullness be the key limiting factor of how long you would spend on the nature walk. What I indicate as a middle way solution is that you can set an alarm clock that would beep well in advance for your next clock bound work-a-day world assignment. Yet, give the clock a brake within that broad time frame chosen for the nature walk; don't let the authenticity of your deep aesthetic experiences be vulgarized by it.

The beauty of life is derived not from the discipline of the chronometer but rather from the timeless consummation of our souls with various time transcendent enriching experiences. Let "*the woods are lovely, dark and deep*" precede the necessitating awareness of "*but I have promises to keep*". Otherwise, the more the outer miles we travel, the more of it will have been taken out of our inner miles.

Seeking Wisdom in a Simulated World

Our imaginations are constantly being seduced by the simulated reality to which we have surrendered our existence. Powerful agencies with vested interests have mastered the principle that the best way to control a society is to overload it with confusing information and then herd its members to a carefully crafted version of the preferred reality. In a situation characterized by information overload, people will intuitively look for the largest information cluster (an information cluster is a grouping of mutually referencing pieces of information) and accept the view of that cluster as 'the truth'.

So, a good strategy to convince people of a particular view (of simulated reality) is to have the mainstream broadcasters bombard the audience with smaller clusters of conflicting views and a significantly big cluster of views that reference well with each other within that cluster. The big cluster views are often salted with emotion-inducing imageries and are repeated for better registration into memory. Powerful corporations (or, even governments) controlling news outlets have done this all along. Jean Baudrillard famously observed that the real Gulf war, the Gulf war that people imagine to be real, did not take place in the battlefield; it took place on CNN, BBC, and other media outlets. The concerted mass media action to discredit smaller clusters of authentic information is evident only to an enlightened micro minority.

What more, over a period of time, our responses to simulated reality become dogmas; these also create real institutions whose existence will then depend upon fostering the simulations as real. If benefiting humans used to be the reason for our institutions once, now it is the other way around: For example, the economy was once thought to mirror society but it has come to a stage where we all agree that the purpose of society should be to keep its economy and the economic institutions strong. Agencies that maneuver public opinion to this end have also been building institutions that ensure continued economic take over of social relations (The latest one: leaked drafts of the Trans-Pacific-Partnership negotiations).

The self awareness of the contemporary man is not at all rooted in the real-reality. Or, we make perfect sense of our lives without ever referring to any such reality. The sense of the simulated world that is being injected into our consciousness provides a comprehensive and self-sufficient quasi-reality within which we find all our meanings for existence and action. We just do not know that this simulated reality is not real and that it is easily and frequently manipulated. Even in those rare situations when we suspect, we don't run away: the offerings of the simulated world have largely made us addicts to its pleasures. Added to this are the confirmatory pressures from our own peers and the threats against defection from the protectors of the simulated design.

While this is not an advocacy paper to exit this complex matrix (there is some 'more beautiful than real' fun in it!), occasionally reminding ourselves of the fact that we are living in a deeply simulated social world is tremendously helpful. It will help us see the patterns the simulation takes, critically reflect upon the vicious grand designs those patterns imply, and prepare ourselves proactively to meet with 'surprises'. Not just in personal lives, but also in our professions.

In my practice as a small business consultant, during strategy briefs, I encourage managers to preserve an 'unadulterated portion of mind' with which to analyse the shapings of the hyper-reality around them. Business research can help us see the big picture behind the scenes only if we frame our analyses with the astute awareness that the data that we gather are drawn from the simulacra. Seeing the reality that lies beneath the simulated existence using the data that we gather from the simulations is indeed a great challenge but not impossible.

A Stoic Alternative to 'Positive Thinking'

If you can't stand the shrill artificiality of the so-called 'positive thinking' philosophy, we are in company.

"Motivation is fleeting: chasing it is a never ending task and its benefits are hallucinatory at the best. Ditch your addiction for the fluffiness of motivation, but rather give 'real life' a life" - It requires some courage to develop a personal philosophy like this to live by. But, in it lies the true freedom that comes from a mindful awareness of unmitigated realism.

Everyday, I remind myself that I am going to encounter a wide range of mental and physical events. I warn myself against anchoring my happiness or sadness upon the perceived goodness or badness of these events, too. I reassure myself that anything that can feast me with an experience is useful: every experience has an inherent beauty, life is designed for the sole purpose of consuming the beauty of experiences, and thus experiences that we encounter in life are valuable gifts.

Since all experiences are valuable gifts, should I not say 'no' to any of them? What if an experience is such that it will become my last of all experiences? What if some of my experiences would mean that I forego the blessings of some other experiences, especially those that I haven't experienced sufficiently yet? What if some of my experiences cause others to forego the blessings of some of their experiences? In summary, what if my chasing after some experiences make me give up the 'moral beauty' associated with the alternate experience of not experiencing them?

Every experience is inherently beautiful. Minimize interpretations of experiences to consume their raw beauty. Adding layers of interpretations make some experiences extremely painful while some others extremely pleasurable. Evidently, most of that range is artificial. Interpretations if any should be limited to preserving the moral beauty of experiences mentioned above. To live is to enrich oneself with the beauty of experiences, but in the morally right way.

I am tempted to label this simple philosophy as a variant of stoicism, adapted for the row man.

Stay happy!

George, Babu P.

A Simple Way to Measure Monoculture in Tourism Destinations

Monoculture is dangerous - both for natural and social systems. Yet, many tourism destinations don't have more than one dominant attraction; or, it is 'planned' to be so.

In economic theory, advocacy for less diversified firms is built upon the premise that highly diversified firms have lower 'general market power' in their respective markets than do less diversified firms. Scale efficiency is touted as the keyword for (short term) profitability and is a killer of diversity. In the name of efficiency, tourism destinations around the world have killed their rich attraction diversity.

Some of our current research focuses upon the consequences of international tourism destinations losing their attraction diversity. The first thing we noticed when we started our investigations in this direction was the conspicuous absence of a methodology to measure attraction diversity. (Isn't it amazing tourism researchers have not yet felt the need to measure attraction diversity in a tourism destination, region, or a country?).

What is Attraction Diversity?

The extent of attraction variance can multifaceted. In its simplest form, it can be seen as variance within an attraction type (or same core product). For example, a destination country may have different kinds of beaches that could be placed on a linear continuum from calm to rough beaches.

B1	B2	B3	B4
C1	C2	C3	C4
Calmest beach			Roughest be

In the above example, different customer types (C1, C2, C4, C4) are attracted to different beach types and the associated businesses (B1, B2, B3, B4) capitalize upon the differences in customer tastes. Another example, even more linear than the one given above, is that of two restaurants serving the same menu distinguishing their businesses based on differences in location and price. Note that perceived diversity need not always match with the numerical diversity.

In a more general way, diversity may be conceived as being composed of three dimensions: variety, balance and parity.

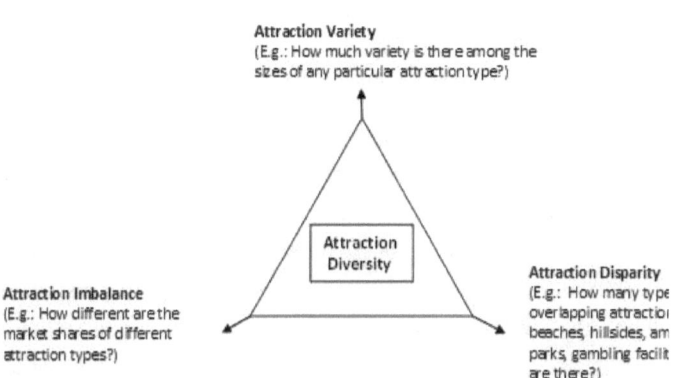

Attraction Variety
(E.g.: How much variety is there among the sizes of any particular attraction type?)

Attraction Diversity

Attraction Imbalance
(E.g.: How different are the market shares of different attraction types?)

Attraction Disparity
(E.g.: How many type overlapping attraction beaches, hillsides, am parks, gambling facilit are there?)

Measuring it

The simplest way to measure attraction diversity is to follow a count approach: diversity can be modeled as $D = N - 1$, where D is a measure of diversity and N represents the number of distinguishable products. For instance, in the special case of a destination with only one attraction, $D = 0$.

The Herfindahl-Hirschman Index (HHI) provides a more robust operationalization of this approach. As you might already know, this index measures the size of firms in relation to the industry and is an indicator of the amount of competition among them (yes, the very HHI being used in antitrust litigations!). That is,

$$H = \sum MS2$$

where MS is the market share of firm 'i' in the industry. Typically, an H below 0.01 indicates a highly competitive, no concentration index. An H below 0.15 indicates a largely un-concentrated index; an H between 0.15 to 0.25 indicates moderate concentration; and, an H above 0.25 indicates high concentration. A good pragmatic approximation for diversity, thus, is the inverse of HHI.

In the spirit of HHI, we propose an **Attraction Diversity Index** (ADI) measure:

$$ADI = 1/\sum (MS)2$$

where MSi represents the market share of attraction cluster 'i' (i.e., revenue generated by the cluster / total tourism industry revenue for the destination).

A Practical Approximation

As we have seen above, attraction diversity index takes into account market shares of attraction types in the selected destination. The operational difficulty here is that revenues and market shares of individual attraction types are not always available. Also, market share for particular attraction types reflects past marketing efforts and tourism policy priorities: misleading figures may result when some distinctly different attraction types do not figure highly on the revenue generation radar. This make us to propose an alternative for market share in the ADI formula: The *Attraction Cluster Equity* (ACE).

In order to calculate ACE, the procedure is as follows:

1. List the top attractions in the destination, using a service like TripAdvisor (www.tripadvisor.com) where travelers rate attractions. In order to ensure 'credibility', you may exclude attractions lacking a critical minimum number of raters.

2. Organize these attractions into one of the known attraction types.

3. Weigh each of these attractions according to the aggregated 'stars' given for them (1 to 5 stars) by the user community.

From these,

Attraction Cluster Equity (ACE) = Weighted value of the attraction type / $\sum$ *Weighted values of all the attraction types.*

To explain this procedure better, let us take the case of a destination country like Jamaica. We classified the top nine attractions to five clusters. We weighed each of these attractions in each cluster with their corresponding star values and then add these values to calculate the relative importance of that attraction cluster.

Attraction Type	Beach & Beach Activities	Cultural Heritage Attractions	Wilderness Attractions	Shopping, City, and Night Life
Weighted Value of the Attraction Type	2 x 4.5 star beaches 3 x 3 star beach activities, 2x4.5+3x3=18	1 x 4 star heritage attraction, 1x4=4	1 x 3 star wildlife refuge 1x3=3	1 x 5 star night life 1x5=5
Attraction Cluster Equity (ACE)	18/(18+4+3+5+4) =.52	4/(18+4+3+5+4) =.12	3/(18+4+3+5+4) =.09	5/(18+4+3+5+4) =.15

Based on the ACE value, we can arrive at a practically meaningful (yet easy to calculate!) measure of tourism attraction diversity by replacing market share with ACE in the original equation of Attraction Diversity Index.

That is,

Attraction Diversity Index (ADI) $= 1 / \sum (ACE)2$

Measurement is the first step towards control. A valid measure of attraction diversity is critical to policy interventions aimed at managing diversity in tourism destinations. Some of you here might find our conceptualization and measurement useful for this purpose.

One More Way to Define Leadership

Long back in 2001, I wanted to do my PhD in Future Studies and not in
Management. My proposal submitted to the Department of Future Studies of
Kerala University was to model leadership along the lines of what is given below.
(Later, I abandoned the idea and instead completed my PhD on an entirely
different topic). I thought to give an electronic life to my original idea and hence
blogging about it:

Let's imagine:

1. Present is like a geometric shape having a large number of tangent lines.
2. Some of these are the tangent lines that connect 'the majority past' with the
present. There could be multiple 'minority pasts' (local maxima), as well.
3. All tangents, including those representing the majority and minority pasts, are
possible futures radiating from the present.
4. Out of all the possible futures, only one will become the actual 'majority'
future, while many others will become minority futures. (Theoretically, it is
possible that there is only one future and that is the all-dominating majority
future; or, there could be the concurrent existence of multiple futures none of
which has a dominating influence). See a simplified pictorization of the same
below (I know, these lines are not drawn as tangents!):

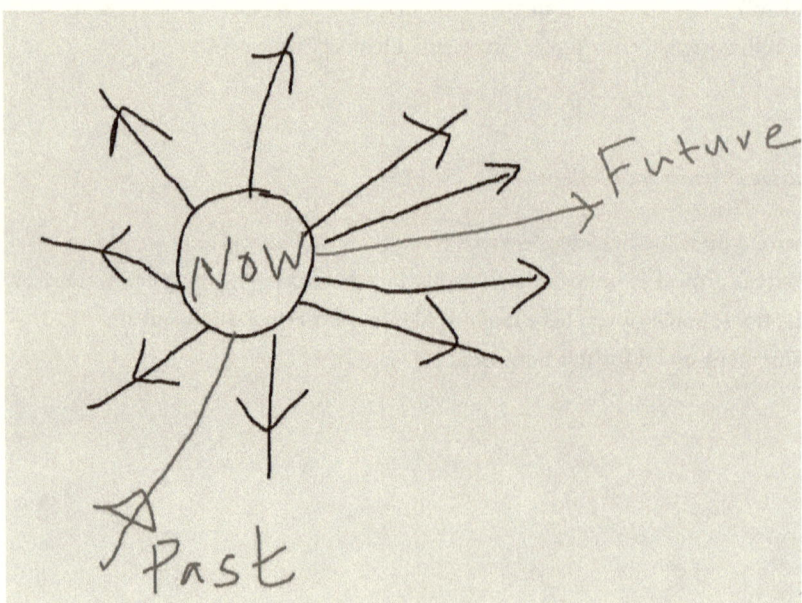

Note: The shape of the present is not necessarily a circle. It could be a deformed
shape in accordance with the density of tangents reaching the present from

various directions. The shape is likely to bulge where tangents from the dominant past touch it and might be lean where insignificant minority pasts touch it. In very rare situations, I can also imagine the present shrunk to a 'point'.

Now, let's try to address the question: who is a leader?

A leader is someone who could see these tangents from the past, how their collective action shapes the geometry of the present, and how, as a result of this particular geometry, tangents to the future are emanated.

Notes:

a. Tangent lines emitted from the present form contours. Majority leaders 'see' high dense areas formed by multiple tangents that are directed to a 'common future', which is yet to be formed. Just as there are multiple pasts, there could be multiple futures, as well. 'Minority leaders' identify some of the tangent-dense areas each of which could be constituting 'local maxima'.

b. Once you identify (envision) the above said dynamics and if you are the only one who could identify them, leadership is like a charm. Articulate the vision you see and take on with you the people who are naturally attracted to it. If there are multiple leaders who could identify the local or global maxima, you may have to share leadership. Elase, some of them who have other leadership capabilities will take over (such as charisma, perseverance, etc). Thus, vision alone is not enough for leadership. Also, may visionaries wish to remain passive than take up the leadership role.

c. Leadership is often a competitive game. Leaders striving to realize a particular tangent maximum might want to bend the nearby tangents and realign these tangents with their contours. Bending could be achieved by the power of ideas or by the power of material forces.

Leadership as being True to the Call of "Thine Own Self".

I have been reading the travel narrative of an otherwise ordinary man who is currently on a journey around the world, experiencing the intimacy of every culture, by road and ferry with no flight segment, with a barebone budget of $30K, all alone. He had been deeply feeling like doing this; he ventured into the trip challenging the norms, the naysayers, and a myriad of other constraints. His journey makes me think of leadership in an entirely different manner.

Isn't this an interesting kind of leadership; or, isn't this *the* essence of true leadership? If leadership is not the willingness, ability, and action with a view to give voice to one's own soul, to help realize its deep felt call, what else it is? Well, I am compromising the notion that the presence of a pool of dedicated followers is what fundamentally defines leaders.

In the past, I have written about leadership oriented to "the other" (e.g. see my LinkedIn post here, which focuses on the vision aspect of leadership). But, I also believe orientation to the other should come only as a desirable corollary to the orientation to the self. Not the other way. Leadership should celebrate the self than annihilate it. If the aforementioned lone traveler's self oriented action inspires us and make us follow his footsteps, that is a meeting point of these two apparently opposed worldviews of leadership.

Remember, this traveler is a true leader primarily because he gave heed to his soul. A thought experiment to explain this: imagine Jesus had virtually no follower when he lived as none else was convinced of his soul's call; but, after a few centuries, he gained millions of followers because time was ripe for his ideals only then. Evidently, it is not those millions of followers who appeared after centuries that defined Jesus' leadership. Followership is a welcome byproduct: an incidental or secondary product, inevitably produced in the manufacture or synthesis of something else.

A lot of times, what we have are pretentious leaders who exhibit themselves to be soul-committed to missions, accumulate followers by seduction, and then misuse them for their vested personal interests.

Marketing to Innovation Laggards: How Marketers have Got it all Wrong.

Some of the earliest references to buying behavior may be found in Everett Rogers' diffusion of innovation literature published in the 1950s. Rogers identified five distinct adopter categories of consumers of technology: innovators, early adopters, early majority, late majority, and laggards. While he never intended to become a marketing expert (Wikipedia identifies him as a communication scholar, sociologist, writer, and teacher), marketing theorists and practitioners both found deep inspiration from his pioneering thoughts. But, did they largely misinterpret the implications of Rogers' classification? I believe so.

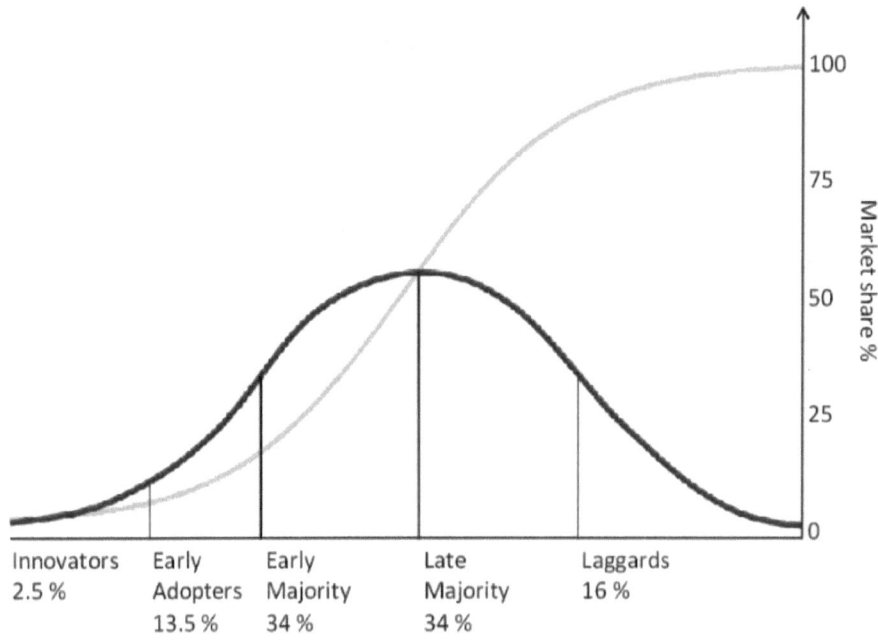

| Innovators 2.5 % | Early Adopters 13.5 % | Early Majority 34 % | Late Majority 34 % | Laggards 16 % |

Rogers prepared his scheme not with the intention of *conversion*. Specifically, he did not want to advance later consumer types to one of the earlier types. However, mainstream marketing experts have interpreted Rogers' scheme as a blueprint for such conversion: marketing success was interpreted as the ability to pull a yet-to-be willing consumer base to buy products earlier in time than they are ideally prepared to. So, if you can make the late majority and the laggards to buy your product along with the early majority or even with the early adopters, the same is counted as pure marketing ingenuity. How awesome that is if we could convert all old people to watch Mickey Mouse before they become sufficiently young, eh!

This is downright gibberish. First and foremost, it disregards the deep personality drivers that make someone a laggard or a late majority adopter. It is no less naïve than saying that you could 'straighten' and 'cure' a gay person by counselling and also the same is a desirable proposition. By marketing engineering (a.k.a. shrewdly combining the 4Ps of marketing), you could make someone *buy* a product but not make him *adopt* it in a personally meaningful way. It is not always hard to see the problem: how ridiculous it would be to inefficiently dissipate millions in promotional expenses to make an unprepared customer segment buy a radically new product only to come to know that the segment does not really adopt it!

Remember, if a product is in the early launch stage and if it requires certain marketing dollars to make an innovator to buy that product, typically, multiple times of that amount will be required to make a laggard to buy it. The inability of such forced users to continue to derive sufficient value from the use of that product often leads to significant negative consequences for the future of that product, too. Yet, the overarching orientation of contemporary businesses for instant results in everything means that such arguments fall on deaf ears.

What if we identify certain groups of late majority and laggard users but never try to convert them? What if we nurture these groups as investments into the future, whom we could tap later in the 'fullness of time'? Begin to foster potential future customer groups earlier on, but don't compel them to buy earlier than they are naturally prepared to. That way, we will have an assured buyer base far longer into the future. The best use of this investment comes when we are faced with product rejuvenation options. Volkswagen probably did not practice this strategy consciously, but the success of the New Beetle may somehow be attributed to such emotional investments.

Some Tips on Life for Young Friends

As I move on, a few things I learned from my life so far:

1. 'Be nice' the way your society wants you to be, but cultivate for you a free space where you can be who you are.

2. Walk at the pace of your life. Don't speed up or slow down too much. Else you will miss the train of your life. You are not born to travel by someone else's train. You will know the ideal pace (and direction!) of your life by referring to the free space mentioned above.

3. Don't try to impress people by any artificial means; there will always be people around you who are naturally impressed by your presence. And, they are the only people whom you should be wanting to be with.

4. If your apologies can make someone happy, just utter those words and move on. Know in your heart that not every war is worth waging, even when you are right.

5. Develop a stoic attitude to life; but keep it only as an emergency source of courage to take out when life deals with you the raw way. The illusion of life is really fun, play it on until you can, and let your games not take away the illusory pleasures of others.

6. Don't worry if your tastes and preferences change over time. You have not promised anyone that you will keep the same body, thoughts, and feelings, from life to death. Actually, be happy when such changes occur since they open up you to a richer variety of life experiences.

7. In order to experience the richness of one year of your life as a teenager, you will need to live two to three years in your thirties. I'm afraid, it must be longer in your forties. You know the implications of this, I'm sure.

Internet Memes and the Shallowness of Management Wisdom

Many of my readers here might already have come across a meme which purportedly shows the conversation between a CEO and a CFO.

CFO: What if we invest in them and they leave?

CEO: What if we don't invest in them and they stay?

The implicit aim here is to highlight the smartness and the strategic thinking abilities of the CEO (in addition to the importance of investing in your employees!). Wow! Isn't it so crystal clear evident that the CFO is point blank wrong? Yes, the CEO's response was more than enough as an answer for most of us and we were fully convinced how right the CEO was.

Created by: Babu George   Made in Cartoon Maker © - www.cambridgeenglishonline.com

Wait! Really? In my view, *the CEO did raise an interesting rhetoric counter question,* *but failed far short of answering a very genuine question of the CFO.* The CEO did not establish why the CFO was wrong, empirically or theoretically.

I am not saying investing in people is not important; my intention here is only to highlight how rhetoric devices and how issues are placed in relative order might impact our personal views irrespective of the factual support for particular claims.

See the following:

Does this second cartoon not help you see that neither the CEO nor the CFO is any smarter? A lot of times, management wisdom is valuable merely because of the shrewdness of the way it is packaged. This is just one of the many examples.

Next time you see a poster like this, take a step back and ask yourself what it smartly hides.

The Octopus as a Metaphor for Organizational Design

The default metaphor when we think of our business (and other social) organizations is the human body. The best of our attempts are to model business organizations after the human body. We believe that the architecture of the human body that gave it supremacy over other known organisms can be mimicked in the design of our business organizations for similar outcomes. One key characteristic of the human organism, like other vertebrates, is a highly localized brain located on 'top' in the head with nerves and muscles acting as command and control lines. Our typical business organizations keep trying to imitate this model, without understanding that the environment surrounding the human organism is not the same as the environment surrounding our business organizations.

An octopus could offer something fresh for the designers of our business organizations. The brain power of an octopus is highly decentralized, making some biologists think it has got close to a dozen brains (and associated consciousness-es). In our traditional business organizations, intelligence is highly localized or, at its best, restricted to certain divisions and hierarchical levels. All other divisions and levels are supposed to follow the orders from the brain center. Even in some of our so-called 'futuristic' designs, those in which decision authority is somewhat decentralized to numerous autonomous units, decision quality still suffers due to the lack of brain resources available to those units. If these autonomous units had sufficient 'neuronal concentration', these could have become more meaningfully autonomous - like the octopuses.

The minds of octopuses are distributed across the body but also work in unison. This offers them the ability to seek multiple perspectives and plan for a wide range of backup alternatives. It is said that they cannot be kept in captivity for long since they often apply their superior contextual intelligence to escape even from supposedly secure tanks. Octopuses have no skeleton, allowing them to squeeze through tight places. No wonder, they are among the most intelligent and behaviorally flexible of all invertebrates. Business organizations need both intelligence and agility. The mind(s) of octopuses are not yet understood in detail; but, I believe, with whatever little we know, octopuses already offer us a vastly improved model for building our business organizations.

Comparing Apples with Bills, Once More.

If you had Googled "more evil than Satan himself" in the year 2000, you would have got a name. And, quite to your shock, that was not Steve Jobs. During the 1990s, Microsoft had the bad reputation of killing innovations and holding small scale innovators, not by better innovations but by their massive market clout. And no doubt, geeks had no better face for the evil than that of Bill himself.

From such rock bottom of public approval, by now, Bill Gates has emerged to become the unequivocally No. 1 messenger of sympathetic capitalism and of corporate charity. And, the crown of evil now, according to most social heat maps, is upon late Steve Jobs. While Bill cleaned up all his dirt with money, Steve used his money for exactly the opposite. I am not saying Steve was unhappy about what he did or he would have been happier if he he had followed Bill's pathway. I am only highlighting how societal imagination about celebrities evolve the way it is.

So, what saved Bill in the societal imagination, in the later course of time? Not his software technology for sure; rather, it is his investments in areas outside of the technological scope of Microsoft. Bill runs a close to $40 billion charity and this made all the difference between him and Steve. Looking from another angle, actually, it is kind of a shame for Bill if it is his social sector investments rather than his technological innovations that became the basis of all his fame. Bill is also valorized in the media (just like another 'charity') for 'saving' Apple with a $150 million infusion when Steve came back to it for a second innings.

To contrast, as emerged from a multitude of tales, Steve is notorious for his 'social-irresponsibility'. Rather, with his "live in my own present, consummate my own life" attitude, Steve could care no less. With his artistic zeal for creative destruction, his entire focus was on disruptively reinventing his business and his own life. He hated to become a stereotypically idealized leader in the popular imagination. In fact, whenever opportunities presented, he actively sought to destroy such 'good' images of him; he felt as though such images would weigh him down from living his own unique call in life. He planted seeds as his heart felt every moment (like learning Calligraphy), knowing deeply within him that sometime in the future he could use their fruits to build an amazing composite ("I used it all into the Mac material design").

Bill 2.0 is the result of his own regret about Bill 1.0. In his own words, as he observed in his Harvard commencement address, "I do have one big regret." Bill 2.0 begins with his new-found conviction that humanity's greatest advances are not in its discoveries but rather in how those discoveries are going to benefit the most needy brethren amongst us. He left the college campus knowing noting of these (An interesting question is whether he would have founded Microsoft the capitalist corporate giant had he deeply empathized with these causes earlier on, before he dropped out of college). Anyway, after decades, he identifies this unpardonable gap in his ken and then determines that the world should henceforth identify him as a crowned champion for helping to alleviate some of the sufferings of the downtrodden. And, if media representation is any true, Bill seems to have won our contemporary society's heart.

Steve 1.0 delighted his customers as much as Bill 2.0 delighted his extra-business stakeholders. Steve did not feel the need for a new avatar later in his life. I believe both have lived their lives fully, in there own ways. But, comparing apples with bills may not be just as easy. The distinct lives of these two men, both born in 1955, stands as yet another proof to the fact that leadership is enigmatic. There is no much similarity between them, other than that they both dropped out of school. But, hey, we are biased to see commonalities, and dropping out of school is thus what determines future leadership success.

Life is Just to Pay the Bills and Die?

The Idealist's Facebook page recently posted this: "*There's no way I was born to just pay bills and die*". Like thousands of others who viewed it, soon it took me to a mood of pensive reflection.

Hadn't I been doing this ever since I was shunted out out of my childhood? Or, even as a child hadn't I been brainwashed to grow up to live a life to pay my bills? Yes, like most of my school - college friends, I too nurtured the notion that I would become an adult worthy of living only from the day I could begin to pay my own bills. Who among us can forget the day we get our first paycheck and the joy of using it to pay our bills for the first time! And, paycheck for us is the key to open the locks to realizing all the thus far unattained individual aspirations; it is the magic wand that could present us with opportunities to live the meaning of life.

This is a trap; most people live paying their bills and die, without even realizing during their lifetime that this is a trap. A trap, executed through various 'global systems' (school, church, mass media, legal system, financial institutions, etc) that trains you for wrong goals it life and those wrong goals then continue to entrap you for the rest of life from you even seeking the right goals in life.

Control is the singular goal of all the global systems straining us from living our own individualized lives. Many of them collude to super-control the lives of those who live at the bottom of the world system pyramid. They are so successful in framing the experience of 'being controlled' as 'success in life' that otherwise well-meaning individuals easily fall into their trap. If you don't have an objective in life that does not fit with the wishes of the designers of these global systems, you are doomed to failure (or, at least so we are taught!).

I see this everyday of my professional life as a professor of business. The highest aspiration of most MBA students is to get a job in a mega-corporation (or, thus they are made to believe, by complementary mega-systems or their local representatives). For this to happen, the students should be able to engineer consumer-employee-stakeholder behavior in ways that maximize their masters' profits. Successful business professors are those who can teach their students how to manipulate customers the best. Student demand for an educational institution's programs depend upon student placements in big corporations, no revenue for the institution without sufficient student demand, and consequently even State funded institutions align themselves with the interests of the single core of the world system.

Is there scope for you to live a successful life beyond the influence of one or more of these global systems? Not only luxuries, but also, increasingly, essential supplies for survival such as food and housing are being controlled by the global systems (or, local systems that are subservient to one of the global systems). Not following their scripted definitions of success is not an option for most of us. Does this mean we are preset to doom or, as *the Idealist* poster implies, accumulate debt to become 'successful' and then work harder until you die to pay those debts?

Is there still space for an 'out-of-the-box' solution for each person born on Earth to construct his or her personal sense of existence in life, uninfluenced by the concocted ethical precepts of the mega systems feasting on our pawned souls? Can we possibly reinvent life in such a way that no one else will bill you for your precious life and that success of your life will not be judged based on whether you are able to pay the debts that you had no choice but to commit?

The Center of the Universe

Asks the Disciple, where dwells the seeds of reality,
In the body, in the world, or beyond?
Smiles the Master with a gesture, strange and queer
Master: Where do you stand? Disciple: On the Earth
And the Earth? In the Universe
And the Universe? In a bigger Universe
And that bigger Universe? In a bigger and bigger Universe
You sure boy? Asks the Master. To this, nodes the Disciple with a sigh
So, what's the size of the biggest container, containing the biggest Universe?
Will finite sizes increase, increase, increase and reach infinity?
And where dwells that biggest container, my dear boy? And you grasp all
that!
Jumps the disciple in ecstasy: Master, I grasped, I grasped it!
Where? Where dwells the roots of reality? Speak to the world!
It's nowhere else, nowhere but in our minds that analyses it all!
We fly to the farthest of the cosmos, but to reach at the deepest recesses of
our minds!
Wow! The biggest container of the biggest universe dwells in human
consciousness!
How simple! How profound! Ain't all profound truths so simple?

There's a truth more profound, though less simple, tells the Master to the
Disciple.
It's not in the mind that you think you have you reach when you run past the
cosmoses
For there is but one truth where all seekers after truth should reach
And a thousand seekers cannot reach a thousand minds as a thousand truths
But all reach at that single cosmic mind - that's what sages say divine
consciousness!
It's but an illusion that we are different: All are one, with space, water, fire,
wind, earth, and us!
But this oneness is not the 'one' of arithmetic, which's learned through
differences!
There ain't differences in divine consciousness! The oneness of it can't be
understood, it's to be experienced!
This is the oneness that include the alpha and the omega: the Word that some
call Om!
This is the mother of all truths: Thou shalt become the centre of the universe
by living this truth!

George, Babu P.

ABOUT THE AUTHOR

Babu George holds a doctoral degree in management studies with a focus on services management and marketing. He has undergone substantial post-doctoral training in interdisciplinary issues that touches upon various social science areas. He has got more than fifteen years of university teaching – research – higher education administration experience (ten years, post-PhD), in the US and internationally. Currently, he is associate professor of management at Fort Hays State University. Previously, he taught at the Swiss Management Center University, University of Nevada Las Vegas, University of Liverpool, Alaska Pacific University, University of Southern Mississippi, and Pondicherry University. He is the editor of International Journal of Qualitative Research in Services (Inderscience).

He serves on the governing-advisory boards of multiple nonprofits working in the social sector, located in various countries. He is a passionate observer of the complex dynamics of creative destruction that makes 'idea innovations' possible. In his free time, he offers free consulting for the budding grassroots level entrepreneurs.

LinkedIn: www.linkedin.com/in/beingbabu

www.ingramcontent.com/pod-product-compliance
Lightning Source LLC
Chambersburg PA
CBHW030013190526
45157CB00016B/2605